Plácido Domingo as Don Carlos, Metropolitan Opera, New York, 1983 (photo: Winnie Klotz)

This Opera Guide is sponsored by

46

Don Carlos /
Don Carlo

Giuseppe Verdi

Editor: Jennifer Batchelor
Opera Guide Series Editor: Nicholas John

Calder Publications Limited
Riverrrun Press Inc.
Paris · London · New York

Published in association with English National Opera

COPYRIGHT DATA

Published in Great Britain, 1992, by
John Calder (Publishers) Limited
9-15 Neal Street, London WC2H 9TU

Published in the U.S.A., 1992, by
Riverrun Press Inc., 1170 Broadway,
New York, NY 10001

Copyright © English National Opera

A Grand Opera with a Difference © Julian Budden 1992

Off the Beaten Track © Gilles de Van 1992

"A Family Portrait in a Royal Household": 'Don Carlos' from Schiller to Verdi © F.J. Lamport 1992

Stendhal's 'Don Carlos': "The most moving opera ever written" © Nicholas Cronk 1992

'Don Carlos' English translation by Andrew Porter © 1992

Italian translations by Piero Faggioni of the French texts published for the first time in the 1980 piano/vocal score © G. Ricordi & Co. reproduced by arrangement

BRITISH LIBRARY CATALOGUING IN PUBLICATION DATA
Verdi, Giuseppe, *1813-1901.*
    Don Carlos.—(English National Opera guides, 46)
    I. Title   II. Series
    782.1092

ISBN 0714542083

LIBRARY OF CONGRESS CATALOGING-IN-PUBLICATION DATA
Verdi, Giuseppe, 1813-1901.
    [Don Carlos. Libretto. Polyglot]
    Don Carlo / Giuseppe Verdi.
    160p.21.6cm—(Opera guide; 46)
    Opera libretto.
    Libretto by Joseph Méry and Camille du Locle originally in French based on Schiller's play.
    'Published in association with English National Opera.'
    Includes the libretto in French and Italian and the English performing translation of Andrew Porter, and commentary.
    ISBN 0-7145-4208-3:
    1. Operas—Librettos.   2. Verdi, Giuseppe, 1813-1901.   Don Carlos.
I. Méry, Joseph, 1798-1865.   II. Du Locle, Camille, 1832-1903.   II. Porter, Andrew, 1928- .   IV. Schiller, Friedrich, 1759-1805. Don Carlos.   V. Series.
    ML50.V484D613   1992 <Case>
    782.1'026'8—dc20   91-32097
                                                                                                        CIP
                                                                                                        MN

English National Opera receives financial assistance from the Arts Council of Great Britain.

Typeset in Plantin by Spooner Typesetting & Graphics, London NW5.

Printed in Great Britain by Billing & Sons, Worcester.

CONTENTS

LIST OF ILLUSTRATIONS

Cover design by Anita Boyd, after Alonso Sánchez Coello
Frontispiece: Plácido Domingo as Don Carlos

A Grand Opera with a Difference

Julian Budden

None of Verdi's operas has so tormented a history as *Don Carlos*. A clue as to the reason can be found in a letter of 1850 from Alphonse Royer and Gustave Vaez, authors of *Jérusalem* (the French adaptation of *I Lombardi alla prima crociata*), in which they tried to tempt the composer back to the *Académie Impériale de Musique*, as it was now called. 'We thought of suggesting to you Schiller's *Don Carlos*. Of course it would merely serve as a point of departure and we should modify it so as to provide you with a scenario that would satisfy you in every respect.'

The term 'point of departure' is significant. Grand opera as evolved by Scribe and Meyerbeer during the 1830s had its own book of rules: a simple action, unencumbered by sub-plots or frequent scene-changes, that moves sufficiently slowly across four or five acts to accommodate massive choruses and ensembles and a central ballet, and in which every act should end with a powerful curtain — an unexpected confrontation, a sudden turn of events, or, best of all, a cataclysm ('effects without causes' as Wagner's jibe has it). Widely experienced in every theatrical genre from spoken play to ballet, from opéra comique and vaudeville to grand opera, and thus able to gauge to a 'T' the special requirements of each, Scribe usually preferred to devise his own plots, if with the help of a collaborator. On the rare occasions when he drew on an existing source, as in his opéra comique *Manon Lescaut* (1856), he never failed to transform it out of recognition. His *Vêpres Siciliennes* (1855), written for Verdi, is indeed based on an earlier piece, *Le Duc d'Albe*; but again the author is Scribe himself.

When in 1865 Verdi decided after all to take up the subject of Schiller's drama, Scribe had been dead five years; but the pattern that he had established remained unaltered. That Verdi was disposed to conform to it is clear from his reaction to the scheme outlined by the playwright Joseph Méry and his partner, Camille du Locle, which his French publisher Léon Escudier presented to him during a visit to Sant'Agata. In a letter to Emile Perrin, director of the Paris Opéra, he singled out for praise two scenes which have nothing to do with Schiller: the meeting of Carlos and Elisabeth at Fontainebleau (an idea derived from Eugène Cormon's play of 1846, *Philippe II, Roi d'Espagne*) and the appearance of Charles V in the guise of a monk — a contrivance that has come in for much critical abuse, especially in Germany, where the resultant dénouement is regarded as an insult to a national poet (indeed more than one German edition of the opera rewrites the text at this point). In time Verdi himself would be uneasy about it. Yet seen in the context of contemporary grand opera, the conclusion as it stands is by no means unworthy of the tradition it represents. Tragedy and transfiguration were alike foreign to the genre. What counted was above all surprise and sensation — Fenella's plunge into a stream of molten lava (*La Muette de Portici*), the revelation that Rachel, already consigned to a cauldron of boiling oil, is Cardinal Brogni's daughter (*La Juive*), the appearance of Queen Marguerite de Valois after the Massacre of St Bartholomew's Eve (*Les Huguenots*), the blowing up of the Palace of Munster during a banquet (*Le Prophète*). That Carlos, surrounded by his enemies, should be drawn into the safety of the monastery by his grandfather, whether living or dead, is not an unfitting climax to a story that has no more basis in historical reality than the legends of King Arthur. Nor is it less fitting that he should be spared a hero's death. Carlos is no Radamès.

'What worries Verdi most,' Escudier wrote to Perrin, 'is the lack of one or two scenes that will really take hold of the public. He would like something unexpected, like, for instance, the skaters' ballet in *Le Prophète*, or the scene in the church — a point of culmination.' It was not the first time that Verdi had harped on that particular string. In 1852 during his correspondence with Scribe about a subject for the Paris Opéra, which would eventually result in *Les Vêpres Siciliennes*, he had written, 'I have constantly in view so many of those magnificent scenes to be found in your poems, among others the Coronation in *Le Prophète*. In this scene no other composer could have done as well as Meyerbeer; but then too with such a spectacle and above all such a situation, so original, grandiose and at the same time so charged with passion, no composer, however devoid of feeling, could have failed to produce a grand effect!' He was, of course, referring to the moment when Jean at the height of his glory is confronted by his mother, and in the presence of the entire populace denies all knowledge of her. Whether Verdi's praise of Meyerbeer was sincere may be doubted, since this is certainly not one of the high points of the score; he himself, one feels, knew that he could have made a far better fist of it, and therefore longed for a similar situation in order to prove as much. The librettists obliged as best they could by building up their scene, in which Carlos draws his sword on his father only to be disarmed by Posa, with the addition of a coronation ceremony and an impending *auto-da-fé* — all strictly in the tradition of grand opera, with no reference to the German play.

Yet right from the start Verdi had wanted to tackle some of the issues raised by Schiller. In his letter to Perrin quoted above he had written, 'I should like as in Schiller a little scene between Philip and the Inquisitor, the latter blind and very old — Escudier will tell you why by word of mouth.' (He has not told us, unfortunately.) 'I should also like a scene between Philip and Posa.' A place was duly found for both, though not where they occur in the original play. In the opera Philip's dialogue with the Inquisitor precedes Posa's death instead of following it, while the long argument between the King and Posa is placed before Carlos's *débâcle* with the Princess Eboli — a fact which seriously confused Verdi when for a revival in Naples in 1872 he revised the ending of the duet with the help of Antonio Ghislanzoni, drawing on lines from an Italian translation of the play, which in their new context made no sense. The truth is that, in aiming at a concept that should exploit all the possibilities of grand opera while remaining faithful to the spirit of Schiller, Verdi had created for himself problems of length and proportion that were not easily solved.

Even by the dress rehearsal these had become all too evident, as a report in the *Gazzetta Musicale di Milano* makes clear:

> Having started at seven o'clock in the evening the show finished around midnight. It is true that the intervals had lasted longer than usual; but even if they had been made as short as possible, the opera would have lasted a quarter of an hour longer than it should have done. In Paris the duration of operas is fixed and the rule cannot be broken. The show cannot go on beyond midnight because the last train for the suburbs and the outlying districts leaves at 12.35 . . . Nor can the curtain go up any earlier since no one wants to make opera-goers hurry their dinner! All these considerations of distinctly menial, not to say downright *slavish* factors have induced, nay forced [Verdi] to shorten the duration of the music by a quarter of an hour.

In the event rather more than fifteen minutes needed to be cut in order to reduce the score to an acceptable length. Act One was shorn of a twelve-minute introduction involving a chorus of woodcutters and their wives

The 'auto-da-fé' in the first production at Covent Garden, 1867 (photo: Mander and Mitchenson Theatre Collection)

together with Elisabeth's first entry: a short solo for Posa and two substantial duets, for Elisabeth and Eboli and for Carlos and Philip respectively, were jettisoned, and the scene between Philip and Posa curtailed. Yet even this was not enough. Before leaving Paris Verdi himself authorised the omission in Act Four of Philip's entry into the prison, Carlos's denunciation of him and the subsequent 'sommossa' (insurrection) quelled by the sudden appearance of the Inquisitor — a typically 'grand opera' touch, this, having nothing to do with Schiller — so that the dead Posa would not have to lie on the ground a moment longer than was necessary.

Even so, it would seem that in its original form *Don Carlos* remained too long for comfort. When in a notorious letter to the press advocating the privatisation of Italy's conservatories Emilio Broglio, the Minister of Education, fulminated against 'interminable operas' and 'Mephistophelean pretensions' he was clearly referring to *Don Carlos* as well as *Mefistofele*, since both had recently made their first appearance at La Scala, Milan. Furthermore, a clause in Ricordi's contract for the hire of the material forbade any cuts under payment of a fine — a condition that could have disastrous consequences, as when the opera was coupled with a new ballet, *Sieba*, at Turin's Teatro Regio in 1878, giving rise to a series of cartoons in the local press entitled 'L'Inclemenza di Tito Ricordi'. Elsewhere the rule was more honoured in the breach than the observance, since the penalty was not easy to exact.

Meanwhile Verdi had already considered shortening the opera with a view to its performance in Vienna in 1875. But it was not until seven years later, with *Otello* already on the *tapis*, that he decided to put his idea into practice. As with the revision of *Simon Boccanegra* (1881) it was partly a matter of getting into trim after the ten-year operatic silence that had followed *Aida*. As well as reducing the total length, Verdi was concerned to recoup as tersely as possible the sense of the discarded passages and to draw the work closer to Schiller and away from the by now outmoded tradition of 'grand opera'. Nowhere is this more evident than in his recasting of the Philip-Posa duet as a dramatic dialogue, once again having recourse to lines from the play. Hence too the removal of a kind of trial scene outside the Monastery of St. Juste preceding the apparition of the Emperor Charles V in the last act ('It was mere note-spinning', Verdi observed; and in any case he had done much the same thing far better in the third act of *Aida*). The ballet was dropped and with it the scene in which Elisabeth and Eboli exchange cloaks and masks, to be replaced by a new prelude. The first duet between Posa and Carlos was reduced by an entire movement. Various internal details were both tightened and enriched. Most drastically of all, the Fontainebleau act was dropped altogether and Carlos's cavatine 'Je l'ai vue' (now translated as 'Io la vidi') resettled in a slightly altered form in the new first act. When Verdi's friend Count Opprandino Arrivabene hinted in a letter that this had been a mistake, the composer replied somewhat testily, 'Of course, those who are forever dissatisfied on principle, that is the subscription holders, are complaining that the first act that they find so beautiful is no longer there; now they say it's very beautiful; before they probably didn't even notice its existence.' As far as he was concerned, the new four-act version launched at La Scala, Milan on January 10, 1884, was in every respect an improvement on its predecessor; it had 'more concision, more muscle and sinew'.

Most of today's Verdians, however, would agree that Arrivabene was right, and for more than one reason. Unless we have heard the first duet between Carlos and Elisabeth at its full extension the subsequent reminiscences of it no longer function as such and the sense of nostalgia is lost. And how much more vividly do we experience Carlos's dejection once we have seen him in the springtime of his hopes! Underlying all this there is a still more vital flaw to be considered.

It will be noticed that when Verdi revises an opera, while he may improve its details a thousandfold, he rarely changes its overall shape for the better. The new pieces in *Macbeth* (1865) sometimes take the shine off the old, so that what was a high point of the earlier score is robbed of its pride of place in the later one. In the revised *Simon Boccanegra* of 1881 there is an inevitable dip in interest after the Council Chamber scene, which takes a while to redress. Even the *Forza del destino* of 1869 sprawls more than its predecessor of 1862, however superior to it in musical content. In reducing *Don Carlos* to four acts Verdi violated a basic rule of music theatre, to which all the great opera composers have always instinctively conformed: that the action should on no account move more slowly in the first act than in the rest of the opera. This is a mistake that Wagner never makes even in the most leisurely of his music dramas (think how much happens within the first twenty minutes of *Parsifal*; or, on a larger scale, in the whole of *Das Rheingold*, which, compared to the rest of the cycle, is *all* action!). Narration, provided it be sufficiently vivid, can prove in part a substitute — see *Tristan* and *Il trovatore*. The first act of *Don Carlos* in its 1884 format is a very different affair. Not only is it extremely long ('not an act,' Verdi remarked at one point, 'it's half an opera!'); in it the action is virtually becalmed. Nothing happens of greater moment than the dismissal of the Countess Aremberg. The remainder is reflection and argument. It is as though a classical symphony were to begin with its slow movement; and the consequence is that, paradoxically, *Don Carlos* in four acts feels longer than it does in five.

Possibly this thought occurred to Verdi himself; for three years later Ricordi brought out a third edition of the opera in five acts without ballet 'allowed and

Tito Gobbi (Rodrigo) and Boris Christoff (Philip) in Luchino Visconti's production at Covent Garden, 1958 (photo: Houston Rogers, Theatre Museum Collection)

approved by the illustrious author', with the Fontainebleau act reinstated, the tenor cavatine restored to its original form and position, and the following acts as in 1884. No correspondence on the subject between composer and publisher has yet come to light; but since this version had already been tried out in December 1886 at Modena — that is, practically on Verdi's doorstep — it could hardly have come into being without his explicit sanction. As well as that, Ricordi published a detailed 'disposizione scenica' (production manual) to go with it, which would indicate that he at any rate considered it the definitive score, since no such manual exists for the four-act opera. True, it was rarely taken up in the years that followed; but by then *Don Carlos* had long given way to the universal popularity of *Aida*, in which problems of length and proportion do not exist. But significantly, it was in the five-act edition of 1887, given during the 1950s in Visconti's production with Giulini on the podium, that the opera first displayed its full glory to a modern audience. No one complained that it was too long or diffuse. Indeed the rediscovery by the scholars Ursula Günther, Andrew Porter and David Rosen of the material of the pieces discarded before the Paris première of 1867, has led to their occasional reinsertion into the later score — not always a good idea, since Verdi had already made good their absence in his final version. But there are two possible exceptions. The spacious introduction to Act One, with its evocation of toil and hardship in a forest in winter, not only establishes from the outset the opera's 'tinta' or colour (to use Verdi's expression), but also helps to account for Elisabeth's heart-broken decision to sacrifice her love for Carlos to the general good. Then there is the Act Four duet for Carlos and Philip with chorus of grandees, which may be felt to explore the emotions aroused by Posa's death more profoundly than the brief exchanges to be found in the revised score. Apart from the inconvenience of Posa's continuing recumbency, there was a further reason why in 1884 Verdi should not have restored this piece: he had already used the same material to very different purpose in the 'Lacrimosa' of his *Requiem*.

Such additions, including that of the Fontainebleau act, inevitably steer *Don Carlos* back towards its origins in 'grand opera'. But this is not necessarily to its detriment. Its peculiar richness, unique in Verdi's works, arises precisely from its dual roots: on the one hand, the grandiose historical fresco of Scribe and Meyerbeer; on the other, Schiller's poignant drama with its wealth of complex personal relationships. To combine both concepts in a single opera was not easy; and there is no blinking the fact that one or two loose ends were left. It is a pity that Eboli's resolution to rescue the Infante is carried out so late, since by the time of the 'sommossa' he has already been set free; nor is it clear to the audience that the riot is her doing; and even her part in it is apt to go unnoticed, with all attention focused on Philip and the Inquisitor. Then there is the question of her adultery with the King. In Schiller Philip has been courting her for a long time; and it is not until she discovers Carlos' love for Elisabeth that she decides to yield to the older man's advances and so gain access to the Queen's apartments in order to obtain, as she thinks, damning evidence against her royal mistress. All this is the more plausible in that Schiller's monarch is not in the least in love with his wife, as he frankly admits. Verdi's Philip, on the other hand, has just sung the deeply moving 'Elle ne m'aime pas', which, of course, would move us a lot less if we knew that the singer had all the while been laying siege to another woman. Therefore the date of his adultery must be left tactfully vague. We can, if we like, imagine it as having taken place before his marriage to Elisabeth. But in that case the punishment inflicted on the erring princess will seem unduly severe, and Elisabeth's horror exaggerated.

Seen in the context of the opera as a whole, however, these are mere trifles. No matter that they preclude the chiselled perfection attained in *Aida*, where 'grand opera' is reinterpreted through the canons of classical drama. But even on the greatest works, perspectives change over the years. For the Victorians the easy confidence of *Ernani*, *Il trovatore* and *Aida* held the greatest appeal. The present age of uncertainty responds more readily to the ambivalences of *Rigoletto*, *La traviata*, *Simon Boccanegra* and *La forza del destino*. Of all Verdi's works none speaks more directly to an age which has seen the collapse of traditional beliefs and values than *Don Carlos*.

Off the Beaten Track

Gilles de Van

Don Carlos used not to be considered a typical Verdi opera: his works were regarded as having been carefully crafted to produce a clear and simple plot, whose narrative line aimed, if not in every detail, at concision and brevity, avoiding scenes that were purely spectacular or episodic. The accepted view was that Verdi had here taken on a genre to which he was unsuited. More recently, the belief that he was constrained by the rules of grand opera, and thereby went astray, has lost favour, and we can now separate where he fell out with the Paris Opéra from what attracted him to French opera.

In fact, there is absolutely no doubt that Verdi wanted to write a 'grand opéra' in every sense of the term, a desire all the more striking at a time when the genre was in decline. Financial considerations played only a small part; but Verdi was certainly eager to triumph in the city that had done so much to enhance the reputations of Rossini, Bellini and Donizetti. But even that was not the real reason — since 1850, Verdi had tried to escape the straitjacket of an artform in which he was perfectly comfortable but that seemed to him too unvaried and too linear. He wanted to use a more complex plot structure and a greater variety of mood, and despite its many limitations, French opera seemed to offer a model for this.

Thus Verdi added to Schiller's play — whose complexity was already well-known — a first act that served as a prologue to the drama, the monumental Act Three finale, the ballet, and even a popular uprising in Act Four. This was a move towards a libretto like those of Scribe, to whom Verdi often explicitly referred and aspired to emulate.

In so doing, the composer had to reconcile two contradictory demands: one to develop the dramatic line with concision and vigour, the other encouraging him to make the most operatically of the scenes which brought a large number of characters into play. From a detailed study of the composer's working methods, it is evident that he was often uncertain and confused, struggling to find a middle way between these two poles. The episode of the popular uprising that follows Posa's death is a case in point: the original version of this scene is rather long and, even before the Paris première, two cuts were made, of 58 and 29 bars (an ensemble on the death of Posa and a solo for Philip confronting the rebellious crowd). It was even proposed that Act Four end at the death of Posa, with the finale completely cut; despite Verdi's refusal to contemplate this, the cut was implemented from the second performance.

When Verdi revised the score in 1882, he wrote to his librettist: 'I don't mind describing the revolt and the Inquisitor's arrival only briefly; but everything must happen very quickly, which creates another problem — sketching out a great and terrible scene, without being able to develop it.' Verdi here admits the irreconcilability of the two demands. As the poet, Montale, noted: 'In this opera, the situation is rarely tackled head-on; it develops and unfolds by successive additions and expansions, giving the impression that it can never reach a conclusion.'

The 1882-83 revision, undertaken at a time when Verdi was already contemplation *Otello* — which he thought of as an intimate Italian work, breaking the mould of his more 'spectacular' works — did not really solve the problem. Certainly, the four-act version 'italianises' the original (from the start, Verdi continually stresses that it must be 'as short as possible') and this emphasis on concision and cutting was in some ways an improvement musically, but even this four-act version, as Julian Budden rightly points out, 'feels its length'.

Verdi was probably aware of this because he never made up his mind on the definitive version, as he had, for example, with *Macbeth* or *Simon Boccanegra*. Having vigorously defended the Paris version — which already constituted a reduction of the original — he set about revising it, less out of conviction than in order not to leave responsibility for the inevitable cuts to anyone else. He seems, however, to have regretted cutting the first, 'Fontainebleau', act.

The opera, therefore, cannot be separated from the grandeur of its original conception: it was to be a 'grand opéra', and was composed and even revised for a French text. Verdi's reservations are understandable considering that this monumentality is the inevitable dramatic result of the need to weave together the private drama (the rivalry between Philip and Carlos, Eboli's jealousy) and the social context of France or Spain. The opera's originality lies precisely in its attempt to represent the interrelationship between individual and community.

The first act[1] demonstrates this clearly. The intimacy of Carlos's romance, or the Elisabeth/Carlos duet — an episode almost unique in Verdi, where two shy young people fall in love — are placed between two public scenes. The first, with the woodcutters, shows the destitution of the French people, exhausted by war. In the finale, the Count of Lerma, in the presence of a large retinue and the people, asks for Elisabeth's hand on behalf of the King of Spain.

The reason that Elisabeth is obliged to give her consent, as the women have begged her to do ('Nous souffrons tant, ayez pitié de nous'/'We've suffered long, take pity on our fate'), is only really comprehensible if it follows the scene with the woodcutters, and if it is clear that Elisabeth was present in the earlier scene. Unfortunately, it was cut after the dress rehearsal and replaced by the much less dramatic call of trumpets and horns to accompany the royal hunt. The fine prelude was also cut, despite the fact that, by using some easily recognisable themes, it clearly established the opera's basic colour [1]. Elisabeth and Carlos are like children who find themselves momentarily free of any social context, in the symbolic space of a forest, only to be crushed immediately by the social space they must inhabit. The gloomy clarinet arpeggio at the opening of Carlos's romance [2], the elegant theme in D*b* with which the duet between Carlos and Elisabeth begins [3], and its first playful and frivolous section, combine to suggest an impossible idyll, that Elisabeth will evoke again in her final aria.

In Act Three, the pivotal scene of the whole drama — the duet in which Carlos mistakes Eboli for Elisabeth, arousing the former's vengeful wrath; a duet that becomes a trio on Rodrigo's arrival [14] — is similarly framed. This violent scene is placed between two units, one consisting of the 'introduction and chorus', followed by 'the ballet of the Queen', the other the grand finale and *auto-da-fé*. This time it is not a varied crowd of woodcutters and huntsmen, but the Spanish court, in all its formality, and with its imposing, sumptuous rituals [15]. In Act Two, plot and spectacle are more smoothly fused: after the sombre opening scene, showing how the Spanish monarchy is weighed down by the Church [5 and 6], comes the elegant tableau of ladies-in-waiting, with Eboli's 'Veil Song' [8]. Rodrigo's 'scène et ballade' serves as much to set up the duet between Carlos and Elisabeth as it does to evoke the pleasantly frivolous atmosphere in which one court gossips about life at another — that of France, which Méry and du Locle could not fail to consider the height of sophistication! [9]

1. Unless otherwise indicated, references are to the version that, after some cuts, was performed in Paris in March, 1867.

The King's study, Salzburg, 1986, with Fiamma Izzo d'Amico (Elisabeth), José van Dam (Philip), Piero Cappuccilli (Rodrigo) and Agnes Baltsa (Eboli) (photo: Siegfried Lauterwasser)

In spite, therefore, of the very real problems of scale that Verdi created for himself, the scope of the work has what Wagner called 'dramatic necessity'. The prison-house of convention and prohibition in which the characters are all trapped is articulated in the scenes with crowds and choruses. And the public dimension is better integrated here than it is in *La forza del destino*, another opera where balance is a problem. The tragedy becomes progressively internalised: crowd scenes are concentrated in the first three acts, and the parameters of the drama are tightened from the start of Act Four. Act Five consists mainly of Elisabeth's aria and her final duet with Don Carlos.

The social context, however, has been elaborated in sufficient detail to keep it in mind even when the characters are isolated in face-to-face confrontation. It is understandable, therefore, that Verdi drastically reduced the rather wordy conclusion of the original version to make a short, violent scene of the kind he more usually wrote. Equally understandable is his reworking of the end of Act Four, which he had first conceived as a moment of spectacle, to enhance its tragic effect: it was reduced to almost nothing in the four-act version. The process operates like a kind of funnel, moving from a public and ceremonial dimension to ever-increasing internalisation.

In its construction, the 1886 'Modena' version is of little interest, because it simply reinstates the first act and attaches it to the four-act 'Milanese' version. However, the Milanese version itself, by omitting Act One — which is merely a prologue, though one that offers the illusion of a dream of freedom — heightens the work's funereal aspect. The tragedy starts and ends in the monastery of San Yuste, before the tomb of Charles V, and opens on the brief and sinister chorus with its reminder that life is nothing but dust [6] — and the last act commences with exactly the same theme in the orchestra.

The prominence given to context raises problems of politics and history in relation to *Don Carlos*. In a famous letter, written in 1883, Verdi listed all the historical falsehoods and inaccuracies in both the opera and Schiller's play, starting with the mysterious monk who turns out to be Charles V and who 'saves' Don Carlos from capital punishment (he only appears in the opera). Verdi always retained this character who had attracted him from the beginning, so it is surprising that the monk's final appearance upsets some producers to the point that they cut it. Verdi was certainly of the opinion that he was dealing with myth rather than historical truth: Carlos, like Idamante, son of Idomeneo, is a mythical character, functioning as the exemplary image

15

of a son sacrificed by his father. But in this case, no voice is heard, as it is in *Idomeneo*, enjoining the King to abdicate. Here Charles V appears and snatches his grandson from a hostile world. He is the embodiment of an ideal of a heroic past that is lost for ever; he is also a representation of death, and no one could construe it as a 'happy end' — what we see is certainly the 'disappearance' of Don Carlos.

This preoccupation with mortality heavily overlays the political significance of the work. *Don Carlos* is political in the sense that all the characters' actions are circumscribed by outside forces. Elisabeth does not accede to the Count of Lerma's request out of some abstract notion of duty, but in response to the pleas of the French people who want an end to war; Carlos does not simply stand aside for his father like a dutiful son — he is obliged to submit for reasons of state. Even Eboli, despite the fact that the political dimension given her by Schiller is omitted by the librettists, takes actions which have political consequences. Thus the political aspect of the opera resides more in the powerlessness of the protagonists to control their fate than in the defence of their ideals.

On this level, Verdi is somewhat ambiguous. Posa is manifestly an anachronism, and his liberalism is no more appropriate in 1867 than it would have been in 1560; the theme of the cabaletta in the second-act Carlos/Rodrigo duet, with its old-fashioned little tune evoking the heroic cabalettas of the Risorgimento, makes this abundantly clear. It is a nostalgic lament, rather than a gesture of hope [7]. Verdi enhances the importance of the Inquisitor, making him brutally implacable as well as grandiose, and his theme describes his heavy and menacing presence [18]. In making him the only really pro-active character, Verdi gives him some of the negative qualities that ought to belong to Philip II, and so makes the King more human and vulnerable.

There is such uncertainty, such fragility, in this character who is all-powerful, yet weak! If the scene between Philip and the Inquisitor was written without revision, that between the King and Rodrigo was revised four times. No doubt it was hard to articulate the political (conservatism versus liberalism) with the personal (Philip asking Posa to help him by observing his wife). But it is striking that there should be three reworkings of the passage where Philip outlines his 'programme' of repression ('J'ai de ce prix sanglant payé la paix du monde'/'Blood is the price that's paid for peace in my dominions'). As the versions succeed one another, the tone becomes ever darker and more bitter:

[C] 1866

PHILIP

16

In contrast to the blind fanaticism of the aged monk, and Posa's lack of political realism, Philip's attitude is one of total disillusion: he tells us that power brings only loneliness, violence and death ('La mort, entre mes mains, peut devenir féconde'/'And death, sown by my own hands, has brought its harvest'). A short passage — in the Act Two duet for Carlos and Rodrigo — clearly demonstrates how such political insights are embedded in the work. Scarcely has the two friends' luminous duet drawn to a close than a solemn march rings out to accompany the royal procession: the pomp of the modern state sweeps away revolutionary dreams. But then this ceremonial music gives way to the chorus of monks reminding us that after life comes death [6]. This juxtaposition suggests the nihilism that permeated the aristocracy.

The tone of the opera, its profound pessimism which dooms the characters to be crushed by the society in which they live, is borne out on the emotional level. *Don Carlos* is a tragedy of powerlessness: powerless Elisabeth doomed to live with a man she does not love, powerless Don Carlos who does not even win the government of Flanders, powerless Rodrigo who dies the victim of an Inquisition more cunning than he is, powerless the King who must bend before the altar and whose power cannot stave off marital disaster, powerless Eboli whose vengeance leads directly to the convent.

It could be said to be common to all Verdi tragedies that the characters find themselves trapped in a situation that reduces them to a state of powerlessness and destroys them. As a rule, these characters keep their integrity and go down fighting. *Don Carlos* is the first work to mark the contrast between the external appearance of social conformity and an interior world of emptiness, solitude and despair. In this way, *Don Carlos* is the precursor of *Otello*, rather than *Aida*, for only in his last tragedy does Verdi go further in his intimate analysis of the fragility of a character destroyed by force of circumstance. It is this that the Italians have termed *Don Carlos*'s 'decadentism', and what could also be called its modernity.

Rodrigo, Marquis of Posa, is the exception. However beautiful his final aria, 'c'est mon jour suprême' ('My last day has dawned forever') [21], however seductive for a baritone his second-act ballade, he remains a character devoid of conflict or tragedy who plainly dissatisfied Verdi to the point that he subsequently considered his function to be 'marginal and purely lyrical'. Eboli, too, is characterised in a somewhat traditional way, in that, when she grasps the consequences of her jealous fury, her internal desolation is partially obscured in the beauty of her music. So it is mainly in relation to the three protagonists that the 'modernity' of the piece resides.

The vocal limitations of the tenor, Morère, no doubt helped to shape the role of Don Carlos, but cannot explain the character's permanent state of vulnerability or the fact that he becomes utterly distraught at the slightest provocation. Take, for instance, his behaviour at the start of the duet with Elisabeth (Act Two). As he struggles for composure, the woodwind melody for his entry halts, suspended in the dominant, and it takes another seven bars to establish a tonic equilibrium. The effort of this proves too great, however, and Don Carlos becomes agitated, as is shown in the violent and tonally blurred accompaniment:

[A]
CARLOS

Then he breaks out in a great cry. This process recurs a little later as he becomes aware of the Queen's coldness. Carlos can only escape from this erratic swing between confusion and crying by recourse to either dreamy lethargy or feverish exaltation — as in the first duet. The pattern is repeated in the second duet, where it dominates the central movement, whether it is in the main theme [10] — the episode that Julian Budden rightly describes as 'a strange visionary trance':

18

CARLOS

or the mild delirium when Don Carlos faints [11]. The indications in the score make this clear: 'in a dying voice', 'in exaltation', 'he falls in a swoon on the grass', 'in delirium'. This ecstatic register is finally fixed in the last movement of the fifth-act duet, in its finely-spun and hovering melody [23]. Nothing could better evoke the profound death wish that haunts Don Carlos, as it does Elisabeth, with a desire to plunge forever into darkness to escape a completely unbearable life.

After the shock of losing her fiancé, Elisabeth shows more self-control than her weak companion. She resists Carlos in their second-act duet and controls her grief in a lyrical and balanced romance. Philip's fury (Act Four) causes her to faint. She recovers only to state that she is a stranger in that land (is she referring to Spain or life itself?). But it is her great scene in the last act that finally reveals her true stature. Her mind is a confusion of memories — of France, Fontainebleau, the Spanish gardens and other dreams — yet, more than anything, she, too, longs for death, for that 'paix douce et profonde' ('God's calm, peaceful and tender') enjoyed by Charles V. Her tragedy is admirably caught by the prelude to her aria, which contrasts the monks' chant with a chromatic theme of deep melancholy:

[E]

Philip II's great monologue at the beginning of Act Four suggests the same inner torment. It is foreshadowed by his Act Two duet with Rodrigo, especially in the magnificent phrase (perfected for 1884) in which Philip reveals to Rodrigo his unhappiness as a husband [13]. In the prelude to his great aria, the six *acciaccature*, the wide-ranging cello solo, the motionless dizziness of the violins, paint a picture, not so much of a coherent emotional state as a

The 'auto-da-fé', Salzburg 1986, producer and conductor, Herbert von Karajan, sets: Günther Schneider-Siemssen, costumes: Georges Wakhevitch (photo: Siegfried Lauterwasser)

devastated inner landscape [16]. In fact, the scene preceding the aria itself evokes nothing but memories, disappointment, regret, frustration, and the King only achieves a continuous melody in his aria when he evokes the eternal sleep that awaits him in the dark vaults of the Escorial.

To express this internal disintegration, Verdi often abandons a traditional melodic construction, where the phrase is built up out of phrase lengths of four or eight bars, in favour of an ample phrase without repetition, which heralds *Otello*. To give an example, the melody may begin with the customary two four-bar phrases, then breaks free to pursue a more capricious or irregular course. This development is the result less of a move towards Wagnerism with its principle of continuous melody (as Bizet had supposed) than an attempt to find an appropriate musical form to express the characters' psychological state — the melody aspires to regularity just as the characters desire coherence, but in both cases, disorder threatens. The characters can only define themselves in terms of the rôle that society has ascribed to them. At the first sign of self-reflection, the façade cracks, and the melody loses its way or is strangled in a cry, as in that great duet between Elisabeth and Carlos in Act Two.

The temporary conjunction, through the melody, of emotional coherence at the psychological level and formal coherence with equal division of the phrase, breaks down and the instability of the characters is mirrored in their mode of expression. It comes as no surprise that the only equilibrium, the only real repose, seems to them to be death: similarly, the most regular melodic passages of the two great scenes for Elisabeth and Philip are the Queen's address to Charles V, whom she longs to join in death [22], and Philip's evocation of his burial place [17]. Life now promises only confusion: it no longer offers the characters a chance to erect statues — death alone permits that, but then only monuments to the dead.

The opera, therefore, is a paradox. It was conceived as a work of spectacle, with its ballet, grand finale and crowd scenes, and this in a sense it remains. But the manner in which it gradually develops destroys this, lifting the veil on those majestic but empty characters. By the end it has become an opera about the loneliness of the human condition, of social alienation, with glimpses of the characters' non-existent inner lives. And it is this that makes it modern.

(The musical themes referred to in square brackets are to be found in the libretto.)

"A Family Portrait in a Royal Household": 'Don Carlos' from Schiller to Verdi

F.J. Lamport

Schiller's *Don Carlos* marks a major turning-point in his career as a playwright. Before it, he had written, in rapid succession, three tragedies, all in prose, but otherwise differing widely in setting and style: *The Robbers, The Conspiracy of Fiesco* and *Intrigue and Love* (alias *Luisa Miller*) — two of which were themselves to furnish scenarii for Verdi operas. The characteristic theme of these plays is the tragedy of idealism: the hero sets out to right the wrongs of a corrupt world, but his own idealism becomes corrupted, or tips over into fanaticism, and he ends up bringing disaster upon himself and upon those nearest and dearest to him, or even (as in the case of Karl Moor in *The Robbers*) upon the wider humanity whose sufferings he had sought to avenge. Something of this can still be detected in the figure of Posa in *Don Carlos*, whose use of deception and intrigue in the service of friendship and humanity helps to bring about the deaths of Carlos and Elisabeth as well as his own, and seemingly does nothing to advance his political cause, the liberation of mankind from tyranny and oppression. This aspect of the play was pointed out by Schiller himself in his *Letters on Don Carlos*, and has been emphasised in some recent productions by Marxist directors eager (to quote one of them) to 'expose the illusions of early bourgeois liberalism'. But it is only a subordinate part in a larger whole. *Don Carlos* marks Schiller's move to a grander and more elevated style than that of his earlier plays, and to the use of blank verse; but above all it marks his discovery of history, which was to furnish the subject-matter of almost all his later plays. Indeed, in the years immediately following the protracted and difficult completion of *Don Carlos*, when he laid aside playwriting in order fundamentally to rethink his conception of the playwright's task, Schiller also turned to historiography, and painted a broader picture of the relations of sixteenth-century Spain and Flanders in his *History of the Revolt of the Netherlands*. For a brief period before the outbreak of the French Revolution — or rather, before the revolutionaries, just like the idealists of Schiller's earlier plays, allowed their noble ideals to be swallowed up in fanaticism and violence — Schiller seems to have been inspired by a faith in historical progress, in the advance of humanity, through a combination of its own efforts and the ultimate guidance of a benevolent Providence, by way of struggle and setback to the eventual attainment of liberty and fraternity.

This was not how Schiller had originally conceived *Don Carlos*, or at any rate described his original conception. '*Carlos* would not be in the least a political play,' he wrote to Baron Dalberg, director of the National Theatre at Mannheim for which the play was originally intended, 'but a family portrait in a royal household.' This was partly, no doubt, intended to reassure Dalberg that the play would not be politically subversive like *Intrigue and Love*, for he had already declared in a letter to his friend Reinwald that he was going to 'pillory the Inquisition' and 'avenge its prostitution of humanity'. But he also wrote, in a preface to the first two acts, separately published in 1786, that although the name of Philip II of Spain was likely to conjure up the image of a 'monster' of tyranny, hypocrisy and cruelty, such a character would destroy the whole foundation of his play. The significance of this remark is rather mysterious, for Philip, as we first learn of him, then meet him face to face, in the first two acts of the play, seems fully to deserve the reputation which posterity (outside Spain) has generally accorded him: that of the embodiment of what Schiller in the *Letters on Don Carlos* calls 'spiritual, political and domestic despotism'. It is, of course, the domestic despotism which provides the plot. In 1559, after the death of his second wife Mary Tudor, Philip married the fourteen-year-old Elisabeth of Valois, daughter of King Henry II of France, who had previously been betrothed to Carlos, Philip's son by his first marriage. Carlos was the same age as Elisabeth. The teenage Prince became increasingly violent and hostile to his father, who finally, in 1567-68, had him imprisoned and, it seems, connived at his death; Elisabeth died a few months later. This much is history, but the fates of Elisabeth and Carlos were fancifully elaborated by subsequent chroniclers — notably the abbé de Saint-Réal, whose 'nouvelle historique' of 1672 was the principal source for Schiller's and, directly or indirectly, for most of the numerous other dramatic treatments of the story. Saint-Réal presents Elisabeth and Carlos as doomed romantic lovers — though he also has an anti-Spanish political axe to grind — and Schiller follows him in this. Schiller seems at first to have identified strongly with Carlos, the dashing young hero who, like Ferdinand in *Intrigue and Love*, finds himself prevented by his father's political machinations from marrying the woman he loves. But it may be that even at this early stage he realised the tragic potential of the King's situation too. As the play developed, and as he studied the historical material more closely — even though his further sources, notably Robert Watson's *History of the Reign of Philip II*, were at least as hostile to Philip as was Saint-Réal — this aspect became more and more important. The finished play has three tragic heroes: Carlos, the romantic lover and rebel against the inhuman father by whom he feels himself despised and rejected; Posa, the idealistic spokesman of those libertarian ideals which Schiller himself held dear, trapped by his very idealism into playing a fatally dangerous political game; and the King, ageing and alone, deprived of human contact and indeed of his own humanity by the despotic role which — as Posa recognises — his position forces him to assume. History moves on, but all three are left behind as sacrifices to its inevitable progression.

Schiller was well known outside Germany throughout the early part of the nineteenth century, the heyday of the Romantic movement. Coleridge addressed a sonnet to the 'Bard tremendous in sublimity' who had written *The Robbers*, and the passionate evocation of the themes of liberty and fraternity in that work (at any rate as they appeared in a French adaptation by La Martelière) earned him in August 1792 the title of an honorary citizen of the French Republic. In the following years he was to turn against the Revolution, declaring in *On the Aesthetic Education of Man* (1795) that an 'unreceptive generation' (he originally wrote 'a corrupt generation') had squandered a great historical opportunity. But he continued to be regarded, quite rightly, as the great modern dramatist of liberty, even if, as Goethe later said, it is 'ideal' rather than 'physical' freedom which tends to dominate his later plays, *Wallenstein, Mary Stuart, The Maid of Orleans* and even to some extent *William Tell*. Again we note that three of these served as the basis for opera libretti, and the opening scenes of *Wallenstein* furnished a number of ideas for *La forza del destino*: the semi-comic Capuchin friar who harangues Wallenstein's unruly soldiers in the play is the direct ancestor of the opera's Fra Melitone. Schiller's plays have indeed much that is 'operatic' about them — vivid, often melodramatic characterisation, powerful confrontations (the ready-made operatic duets of which *Don Carlos* contains some of the finest examples) and noble sentiments passionately expressed. They were also seen by continental dramatists of the period as highly suitable models for the revitalisation of the dramatic genre which they felt to be so necessary after

The 'auto-da-fé', Cologne, 1964; producer, Arno Assmann, set designer, Max Bignens, costume designer, Sophia Schroeck (photo: Stefan Odry)

centuries of domination by the restraints of the neo-classic style. From *Don Carlos* onwards Schiller himself had aimed to strike a balance between the unconstrained 'Shakespearian' freedom which he had espoused in *The Robbers* and the discipline and formal balance of the classical manner.

In France, Schiller's plays were translated and adapted by various hands; Benjamin Constant's adaptation of *Wallenstein* (1809) was particularly significant. But the major part in promoting German literature in France was played by Madame de Staël's *De l'Allemagne* (1814), and her praise of Schiller inspired many writers of the Romantic movement proper, notably Victor Hugo. Hugo knew no German and had to read Schiller in translation, but there are Schillerian echoes in many of his plays, in *Hernani* and *Ruy Blas* in particular — some of which found their way back into Méry and du Locle's adaptation of *Don Carlos*. In Italy Schiller was not so highly regarded, being often unfavourably compared with his near-contemporary Alfieri, another playwright devoted to libertarian ideals. (Carlyle also thought that Alfieri's neo-classic *Filippo* of 1775 was better than Schiller's *Don Carlos*.) Schiller was, however, championed by the great Romantic patriot and republican, Mazzini. In his essay *On Historical Drama* of 1830 — the year he was forced to go into exile from Italy — he praises *Don Carlos* enthusiastically, as of all Schiller's works the one most perfectly inspired by love, by youthful ardour, by his heart and his genius, by his spirit which was the 'foco di belle e generose passioni', by his ideals which were to become the 'religion of the future'. Again in his address *To the Poets of the Nineteenth Century* (1832) he urges his compatriots to espouse a revolutionary and progressive spirit, the 'vita, moto, foco d'azione' which are found in such models as 'Schiller, Dante, Alfieri'. And in *Faith and the Future* (1835) he recalls *Don Carlos* again in attacking 'authority blind and deaf like Schiller's Inquisition'. A complete Italian translation of Schiller's

Raina Kabaivanska (Elisabeth), Ettore Bastianini (Rodrigo) and Grace Bumbry (Eboli), Metropolitan Opera, 1965 (photo: Louis Mélançon)

plays was made in the 1840s by Andrea Maffei. Verdi had met Mazzini in London in 1847, and knew Maffei well; as early as 1849 he drew his librettist Cammarano's attention to *Wallenstein* in connection with their unrealised project *L'assedio di Firenze*. On the other hand, *Luisa Miller*, completed in the same year, is barely recognisable as having anything to do with Schiller. *Don Carlos*, however, shows evidence of a close study of Schiller's play on Verdi's part.

Méry and du Locle did make a number of significant changes in their adaptation. The whole first act in Fontainebleau is an addition (derived from a French play on the subject, Eugène Cormon's *Philippe II, roi d'Espagne* of 1846), which provides a more effective and theatrically vivid exposition; in Schiller, the betrothal of Carlos and Elisabeth and the intervention of Philip are narrated in retrospect. They also effectively simplified and restructured Schiller's excessively, indeed at times impenetrably, complicated plot, and in the opera the course of the action is much more easily comprehensible. Major additions are the *auto-da-fé* in Act Three, with the heavenly voice promising the victims peace and deliverance, and the appearance of the Monk/Emperor in Acts Two and Five. Schiller's first act ends with the confrontation of King and Queen in the garden, the banishment of Mondecar (Aremberg in the opera) for leaving the Queen unattended, and the King's summoning all his court — after the Queen has expressed her horror of such scenes — to witness an *auto-da-fé* which, he brutally declares, shall be on an unprecedented scale; but we do not see the *auto-da-fé* on stage. In the opera it certainly furnishes the

24

theatrical spectacle which Verdi thought lacking when he first considered *Don Carlos* as an operatic subject. The supernatural interventions are more questionable, introducing as they do an element which is completely absent in Schiller. In the play the final encounter between Carlos and the Queen takes place in her apartments in the royal palace: Carlos gains access by disguising himself as the ghost of the Emperor which is, we are told, *rumoured* to haunt the palace in the form of a monk. The ghost-story motif adds an appropriate hint of fatality to the last act of the tragedy, but in the opera the actual appearance of the Emperor's spirit introduces, as in the *auto-da-fé* scene, a motif of redemption and deliverance on a supernatural plane, whereas in the play the tragedy of Carlos, Posa and the Queen, and of the ideals which all three espouse, is 'redeemed' rather by the prospect of historical progress. In both the *auto-da-fé* and the final scene of the opera the supernatural interventions suggest the hand of a loving God, and the vengeful brutality of the Inquisition appears as a perversion of true religion and spirituality; in Schiller's play the Inquisition is seen rather in secular terms, as an affront to humanity and as the sustaining power of earthly tyranny and oppression. In the opera the specifically political force of Schiller's play is thus arguably muted.

However, the two great political dialogues, between the King and Posa and between the King and the Grand Inquisitor, are both based closely on Schiller, and were included in the opera on Verdi's insistence: they did not appear in Méry and du Locle's original draft libretto. In both play and opera they are designed to balance each other closely: the King listens first to the voice of humanity and liberation, then to the voice of unflinching repression. Posa is (together with Carlos, but on a more reflective, abstract level) the spokesman of the future; the aged, blind Inquisitor is the voice of reaction, of death and

Juan Lloveras (Don Carlos), Nicolai Ghiaurov (Philip) and Mirella Freni (Elisabeth), Houston Grand Opera, 1982 (photo: Jim Caldwell)

Set design for the King's study by Caspar Neher, for Frankfurt am Main, 1941 (photo: Stadtarchiv Frankfurt am Main)

decay. 'For whom then have I garnered?' asks Schiller's King, to receive the terrifying, uncompromising reply 'For decay, rather than liberty'. But the two scenes also encapsulate, as Verdi must have realised, much of the personal tragedy of the King, caught between the generations, between youth and age. It was an invention of Schiller's, which Verdi again expressly insisted on following, to make the Inquisitor ninety years old and physically enfeebled. In historical fact, Carlos at the time of his death in 1568 was 23, Philip his father was 45, and the Grand Inquisitor, Cardinal Espinosa, was in his mid-sixties; Schiller emphasised the symbolic significance of the conflict of the generations by widening the age-gap to over thirty years in each case. Philip, the father estranged from his son, seeks a substitute in Posa, but is forced to sacrifice them both to his 'spiritual father'. For Schiller this reversal of the course of nature symbolises the futility, in the longer term, of resisting the force of historical progress. In the opera the Inquisitor's usurpation of the father-role is highlighted by the final appearance of the Emperor, Philip's actual father: true paternity is restored, though again, it seems, only in a world beyond this one. Perhaps the opera more truly than the play deserves the title of a family portrait rather than a political drama.

Verdi at first approved of the librettists' introduction of the Emperor's ghost, though he seems later to have had doubts about it. His later revisions, including the cutting of the first act, all seem designed to bring the opera back closer to the Schillerian original. He wrote in 1883 that the four-act Italian version had 'più concisione e più nerbo', more concision and more strength or sinew. The phrase curiously recalls one of Schiller's first remarks about the play, exactly a hundred years previously, when he had written to Reinwald that his Carlos would draw 'from Shakespeare's Hamlet his soul, from Leisewitz's Julius [another soulfully rebellious 'Sturm und Drang' hero] his blood and sinews ['Nerven'], and his pulse from me'.

Stendhal's 'Don Carlos':
"The most moving opera ever written"

Nicholas Cronk

Don Carlos is, of course, a French opera in conception, and although Verdi's librettists used Schiller as their primary source, Méry and du Locle were clearly well-acquainted also with the French novel which had been Schiller's primary source, Saint-Réal's *Don Carlos*. The abbé de Saint-Réal (1639-1692) is now a forgotten figure, but in the eighteenth and nineteenth centuries his writings were widely praised and often reprinted. Of all his admirers, none was more enthusiastic than the novelist Stendhal — who was also a great lover of music, especially after the revelatory experience of hearing Cimarosa's *Il matrimonio segreto* in 1800. In a remarkable passage of his *Journal* dating from 1804, Stendhal imagines the opera libretto he could write based on Saint-Réal's *Don Carlos*, a work which had already inspired several French stage plays (by Le Fêvre, 1784, and Mercier, 1785) in addition to the better known works by Otway (1676) and Alfieri (1783), but no operas. Stendhal's libretto was never written (though in 1816 he did try his hand at another, *Il forestiere in Italia*, which he left unfinished), perhaps sensing that no contemporary composer — Boieldieu? Méhul? Cherubini? — would have been adequate to the task: Rossini was too young. The musician in Stendhal does all the same appear to have grasped the operatic potential of Saint-Réal's *Don Carlos*, and fifty years before Verdi.

5 thermidor, year XII [24 July, 1804]

[. . .] Thinking of the absurdity of *Le Connétable de Clisson* [an opera by Porta, words by Aignan, first performed in Paris in 1804], I thought one could make a good three-act opera out of *Don Carlos*. You would show magnificent celebrations and, in the midst of these staged miracles, Philip II, an appalling tyrant, and Carlos, like Elisabeth, lost in love; you would show them disconcerted by the pomp of their surroundings. I would console men for not being kings by showing how much their greatness often irks them, and how much the sadness of Elisabeth's sensitive soul is compounded by her being forced to appear calm when her heart is in despair. I would show her loathing her grand surroundings and yearning for obscurity. This aspect of royal love is new. The principles of the work would be essentially republican and all the more effective because words like 'Patrie' and 'Vertu' would remain unspoken. The character of Elisabeth could be a most touching role, and my opera one of the most moving ever written. The ballet scenes could be integrated in a perfectly natural way, in the marriage of Don Carlos and Elisabeth, or of the King, depending on which plan I adopted; the three characters would not just be passive spectators of the ballet scenes, which would be punctuated with a sign, a word, the passing of a letter or the comment of a spy. This would enliven those parts which are always dull and the whole effect would be delightful. I saw a modest example of this in *Figaro*, which they played two years ago at the Opéra [. . .].

27

Ruggero Raimondi (Philip) and Carlo Cossutta (Don Carlos), Bayerische Staatsoper, Munich, 1987 (photo: Sabine Toepffer)

Don Carlos

Grand Opera in Five Acts by Giuseppe Verdi

Text by Joseph Méry and Camille du Locle
after the dramatic poem *Don Carlos, Infant von Spanien*
by Friedrich Schiller

Italian translation by Achille de Lauzières
and Angelo Zanardini, with additional material
translated by Piero Faggioni

English translation by Andrew Porter

The first performance of *Don Carlos* was at the Académie Impériale de Musique (Opéra), Paris on March 11, 1867. The first performance in Britain was at Covent Garden, London, on June 4, 1867, in the Italian translation by Achille de Lauzières. The first performance in the United States was in New York on April 12, 1877 (in Italian). The revised version (reduced to four acts) was first performed (in Italian) at the Teatro alla Scala, Milan, on January 10, 1884. The first performance of this version in the United States was in New York on December 23, 1920 and its first British performance was at Covent Garden on June 1, 1933. The first English-language production was at Sadler's Wells, London, on December 6, 1938 (in a translation by S. Austin). Andrew Porter's singing translation was first performed in a new production by English National Opera at the London Coliseum on August 21, 1974.

Introduction

Jennifer Batchelor

This libretto follows the complete score prepared for Paris in 1866/67, as reconstructed by Ursula Günther and Luciano Petazzoni, and published by Ricordi in 1980. The French libretto by Joseph Méry and Camille du Locle for a 'grand opéra', in five acts with a ballet, includes those passages cut before the 1867 première, and lost until the 1970s.

For the most part, the Italian text is the translation by Achille de Lauzières and Angelo Zanardini, given according to Verdi's revisions for three nineteenth-century productions of the opera in Italy — Naples 1872, Milan 1884 and Modena 1886. (The opera was first performed in Italian at Covent Garden, London, in June 1867, in a translation by de Lauzières.) Because Verdi never reinstated the cuts made before the Paris première, however, these passages were not translated into Italian at the time and were first published in

The 'auto-da-fé', Salzburg (photo: Bildpressedienst Salzburg)

an Italian singing version by Piero Faggioni in the 1980 Ricordi piano/vocal score.

As Verdi worked on the opera over twenty years, he made many revisions to both music and text, not only for aesthetic and dramatic reasons, but because of length. Of the four principal versions (i.e. Paris, Naples, Milan, Modena), Naples is the one that remains closest to the Paris original. When changes for Naples necessitated an Italian text (for the Posa/Philip duet, for example), this was freshly supplied by Antonio Ghislanzoni.

The version which contains the most substantial changes from Paris is the one Verdi prepared for Milan. This is the version in four acts (it excludes the opening 'Fontainebleau' act) and its Italian text is the one that has been most frequently performed. New material was supplied by du Locle and translated by Zanardini, and the previous translation by de Lauzières was revised as necessary by Zanardini. Even when Verdi was working on the Italian versions, he generally used the French libretto, and these revisions then had to be translated. The Modena version reverts to the five-act schema. It reinstates the Paris first act and its opening of Act Two, scene one: thereafter it is identical to the Milan version.

The English text is the translation by Andrew Porter, made for a production by ENO in 1974. He has supplemented this with translations, some singing, some literal (which are indicated by square brackets in the text), of the passages which were not performed then.

The libretto reflects the Paris score, rather than the French printed libretto of 1867, and it does not, for reasons of space, follow the elaborate indentations of the latter, though it does follow its lineation. Nor does it break up the libretto into scenes in the traditional French manner: it follows the pattern given in the score. It does not contain lines which were never set to music, nor the many instances where the librettists' original lines have been modified by the composer. Notes of interesting variants from the printed libretto are here prefaced by the sign §.

The numbers and letters in square brackets refer to the musical themes and examples in Gilles de Van's essay.

In 1867, a *Disposizione Scenica* for the Paris production was published. Diagrams and information (from the third edition, 1884) with details about characterisation, sets and staging are also included in the notes.

Any production of the opera can offer only a possible reading of the opera, following one of the four versions mentioned above, or drawing on more than one, and on material cut before the première. This libretto provides a way through most of the text that is ever likely to be used in a production or recording of *Don Carlos*.

31

Philip II, *King of Spain*	Philippe II
Don Carlos, *heir to the throne of Spain*	Don Carlos
Rodrigo, *Marquis of Posa*	Rodrigue
The Grand Inquisitor	Le Grand Inquisiteur
A Monk	Un Moine
Elisabeth of Valois	Elisabeth de Valois
The Princess Eboli	La Princesse Eboli
Thibault, *page to Elisabeth of Valois*	Thibault
A Heavenly Voice	Une Voix d'en Haut
The Countess of Aremberg	La Comtesse d'Aremberg
A Woman in Mourning	Une Femme en deuil
The Count of Lerma	Le Comte de Lerme
A Royal Herald	Un Héraut royal
Flemish Deputies	Députés flamands
Inquisitors	Inquisiteurs

Lords and Ladies of the Courts of France and Spain, Woodcutters, The People, Pages, Guards of Henry II and Philip II, Monks, Officials of the Inquisition, Soldiers.

The first act is set in France, the others in Spain, around 1560.

The Queen's garden at night, Salzburg, 1979, with Agnes Baltsa (Eboli), Piero Cappuccilli (Rodrigo) and José Carreras (Don Carlos) (photo: Siegfried Lauterwasser)

Filippo II	*bass*
Don Carlo	*tenor*
Rodrigo	*baritone*
Il Grande Inquisitore	*bass*
Un Frate	*bass*
Elisabetta di Valois	*soprano*
La Principessa Eboli	*mezzo-soprano*
Tebaldo	*soprano*
Una voce dal Cielo	*soprano*
La Contessa d'Aremberg	*[silent]*
Una Donna in lutto	*[silent]*
Il Conte di Lerma	*tenor*
Un Araldo reale	*tenor*
Deputati fiamminghi	*basses*
Inquisitori	*basses*

The 'auto-da-fé', Metropolitan Opera, 1971, with Martina Arroyo (Elisabeth), Plácido Domingo (Don Carlos), Robert Merrill (Rodrigo) and Cesare Siepi (Philip) (photo: Louis Mélançon)

Act One *

Prelude and Introduction. [1] †

Scene One. *The forest of Fontainebleau. Winter. The palace in the distance. On the right, a large rock forms a kind of shelter. Woodcutters, their women and children. Some chop at fallen oaks, others cross the stage carrying faggots, pieces of wood and tools. The women and children warm themselves at a lighted brazier beneath the large rock.*

WOODCUTTERS AND THEIR WOMEN

The cold is keen! We face starvation!	L'hiver est long! La vie est dure!
Our life is hard. How long will it last,	Le pain est cher!
Icy winter, O Lord, how long?	Quand donc finira ta froidure,
Alas! When will the war be over?	O sombre hiver!
When can we hope to see all our sons	Hélas! Quand finira la guerre?
Return home again and find our garners	Hélas! Reverrons-nous jamais
Filled with grain? Alas! Alas!	Et nos fils dans notre chaumiére
The cold is keen! We face starvation!	Et des blés mûrs dans nos guérets?
All dies, our crops have been killed by frost,	Tout meurt au bois, dans la plaine
Our beasts have died in the snow.	L'eau des fleuves manque aux troupeaux
And the winter has laid its icy grasp	Et l'hiver glace la fontaine,
On the streams of Fontainebleau.	Notre fontaine aux belles eaux!

A WOODCUTTER

Good friends, now return to your labour.	Amis, hâtons-nous à l'ouvrage!
May the courage of those who have gone to fight	Que nos femmes, nos fils, nous donnent du courage!
Inspire us when peace returns,	Avec la paix, ô travailleurs,
Then we shall know bright days of joy once more!	Nous reverrons des jours meilleurs!

WOODCUTTERS

But hear the call! The trumpet's sounding.	Entendez-vous? Les trompes sonnent!
I hear the horns. The call is sounding.	Entendez-vous? Les cors résonnent!
The Court's riding out in our woods.	La cour a quitté le palais!
Are the huntsmen coming this way?	Le Roi chasse dans nos forêts!

HUNTSMEN *in the distance*

The stag flies fast,	Le cerf s'enfuit sous la ramure . . .
But he will not escape us!	Par Saint Hubert!
For we'll pursue until we catch him.	Suivons-le, tant que le jour dure,
Halù! Halà!	Au bois désert!

[1] ACT ONE - Prelude

34

* This Act is completely absent in the four-act Milan version of 1883/84.

† This opening passage was cut before the Paris première in 1867, which began with the sounds of the hunt before the appearance of Don Carlos.

‡
L'inverno è lungo! La vita è dura!
Il pane è caro!
Mai più finirà il tuo gelo,
O inverno amaro!
Ahimè! Terminerà la guerra?
Ahimè! Li rivedremo mai? Rivedremo
    ritornare
I figli nostri ai casolari
E i campi arati maturar?

Qui di freddo e fame si muore

E giù al piano il fiume ghiacciò.
Dell'inverno il gran rigore
L'acque gelò di Fontainebleau!

‡ Because this passage was cut before the Paris première, it was not included in the translation of the French libretto into Italian by Achille de Lauzières and Angelo Zanardini. The Italian for this and the other deleted passages was supplied by Piero Faggioni.

Amici, ritorniamo al lavoro!
Per le spose, i figli, facciamoci coraggio!

La pace a noi lavoratori
Ridonerà dei dì migliori.

Sentite là? La tromba chiama!

Sentite là? Risponde il corno!
La corte a caccia verrà!
Della caccia il Re sarà!

Su, cacciator! pronti o la belva
Ci sfuggirà!
E noi l'avrem, pria ch'alla selva
Notte verrà.

Diagram of Act One from the 'Disposizione Scenica': 1. Backcloth in the distance showing the royal palace in the snow; 2. A wooded hill; C represents a large rock; D is an outcrop of land reaching towards F forming a kind of cave; X is a small bench; Y is a brazier. Spread on the stage is a cloth painted like snow with the imprints of footsteps and tracks, etc..

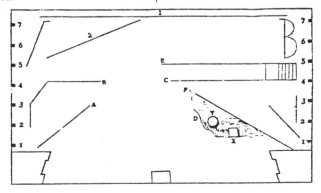

WOODCUTTERS

I hear the voices drawing closer,	Le son du cor de nous s'approche!
The huntsmen set the echoes flying!	Il retentit de roche en roche!
The air is filled with joyous cries!	L'air est plein de leur bruit joyeux!
Free from care the life of a king!	Que le sort des rois est heureux!

Elisabeth appears left, on a horse, led by Thibault, her page. Attendants and pikemen.

WOODCUTTERS AND THEIR WOMEN

See our Princess herself. Hurry, let us go to meet her.	C'est la fille du Roi! Vite, approchons-nous d'elle!
She'll hear us, if we all entreat her.	Elle est aussi bonne que belle!
Elisabeth is kind.	La noble Elisabeth . . .

ELISABETH *stopping her horse amid the woodcutters* ◊

My friends, what would you ask?	Amis, que voulez-vous?

WOMEN *leading a woman in mourning to Elisabeth*

No favour for ourselves we'd ask,	Nous ne demandons rien pour nous,
But can you help this mother here,	Mais secourez dans sa misère
This grieving widow who's lost two sons.	Cette veuve dont les deux fils,
To save your land they went to war.	Sous l'étendard du roi partis,
Ah! They did not return.	Ah! ne sont pas revenus!

ELISABETH *to the poor woman*

Oh, mother, Let me give to you this golden chain.	Ma mère, Je te donne ma chaîne d'or . . .

to the woodcutters

And, my friends, we can hope that now the cruel war	Et vous tous, espérez! Bientôt la triste guerre
Is at an end, fair days of calm will soon return.	Finira. De beaux jours pour nous luiront encor!
At the Court of the King, my father,	Vers le Roi Henri deux, mon père,
Ambassadors from Spain have arrived.	Un envoyé d'Espagne est venu . . . De la paix
And if God so wills, they'll sign the peace;	Bientôt, s'il plaît à Dieu, renaîtront les bienfaits!
Once again fair peace will bless this land.	

WOODCUTTERS AND THEIR WOMEN

Noble lady, we pray that God is kind,	Noble dame, que Dieu vous donne,
And grants that prayer our hearts desire,	Dans notre coeur lisant nos voeux,
And guides your path to a glorious throne,	Un jeune époux, une couronne,
And fills your days with joy and love.	Avec l'amour d'un peuple heureux!
When peace returns, then we shall know	Avec la paix, ô travailleurs,
Bright days of joy once more.	Nous reverrons des jours meilleurs!

Elisabeth smiles, salutes the chorus, and leaves, right, with her suite, to the sound of hunting horns. Don Carlos appears on the left, concealing himself amid the trees.

HUNTSMEN

The stag flies fast,	Le cerf s'enfuit sous la ramure . . .*
But he'll not escape us!	Par Saint Hubert!
Halù! Halà!	Suivons-le, tant que le jour dure,
For we'll pursue until we catch him!	Au bois désert!

WOODCUTTERS AND THEIR WOMEN

Ah! When peace returns, then we shall know	Avec la paix, ô travailleurs,
Bright days of joy once more.	Nous reverrons des jours meilleurs!

The woodcutters watch the Princess's departure, take up their tools, make their way off, and disappear back left.

Il suon dei corni s'avvicina,
Echeggian grida d'ogni parte;
Chi più di lor felice è?
Fortunata è la sorte dei re!

È la figlia del Re! Presto, ci appressiamo
    a lei!
Non è meno buona che bella!
La nobile Elisabetta . . .

◊ According to the *Disposizione Scenica*
Elisabeth is 'in Act One elegant, gay —
then sad and lost at the severe Spanish
court, lamenting the loss of her
homeland, but keeping alive her finest
feelings.'

                    Amici, che mi chiedete?

Noi non vi supplichiam per noi,
Ma soccorrete la miseria
Di questa vedova i cui due figli
Chiamaci in guerra per il Re,
Ah! non tornarono più!

                    Accetta,
Buona madre, questa catena d'or . . .

E voi tutti, sperate! Ben presto questa
    guerra
Finirà. Dei bei dì per noi verranno
    ancora!
Presso Re Enrico, mio padre,
Un messo il Re di Spagna inviò . . . Con
    la pace
Ormai, se Dio vorrà, tornerà la serenità!

O Signora, che Dio vi doni,
Leggendo in fondo al nostro cuor,
Un giovin sposo e la corona
E d'un popolo l'amor!
La pace, a noi lavoratori
Donerà dei dì migliori!

‡
Su, cacciator! pronti o la belva
Ci sfuggirà!
E noi l'avrem, pria ch'alla selva
Notte verrà.

* The version of the opera performed at
the Paris première in 1867, and the
Italian-language versions done for
Naples in 1872 and Modena in 1886, all
commence here.

La pace a noi lavoratori

‡ It is here, too, therefore, that the de
Lauzières/Zanardini translation begins.

Ridonerà dei dì migliori.

Recitative and Romance.

DON CARLOS *alone* ◊

Fontainebleau! You gloomy woods, immense and lonely!
Far more dear than the flowers of all the brightest gardens,
Is this cold frozen ground, branches so bleak and bare,
Which my Elisabeth has transformed by her smile!
By leaving Spain and the Court of my father,
Unafraid of his wrath and his stern cruel anger,
And all unknown among the Count of Lerma's train,
At last my eyes have seen the smile of my beloved,
She who has ruled my thoughts since first our hands were plighted,
She who forever more now will rule in my heart!

Here I saw her, here I was captured,
And her smile gently stole my heart.
Now, with joy, I read all my future,
From her beauty I'll never part.
Ah, sweet future shining before us,
Joy foretold by bright stars above!
God has smiled on two youthful lovers,
God will bless our pure tender love!

Fontainebleau! Forêt immense et solitaire!
Quels jardins éclatants de fleurs et de lumière
Pour l'heureux Don Carlos valent ce sol glacé
Où son Elisabeth souriante a passé?
Quittant l'Espagne et la cour de mon père,
De Philippe bravant la terrible colère,
Caché parmi les gens de son ambassadeur;
J'ai pu la voir enfin, ma belle fiancée,
Celle qui dès longtemps régnait dans ma pensée,
Celle qui désormais régnera dans mon coeur!

[2] Je l'ai vue, et dans son sourire,
Dans ses yeux pleins d'un feu charmant,
Tout ému, mon coeur a pu lire
Le bonheur de vivre en l'aimant.
Avenir rempli de tendresse!
Bel azur dorant tous nos jours!
Dieu sourit à notre jeunesse,
Dieu bénit nos chastes amours!

Scena and Duet.

Don Carlos sets out in the direction taken by Elisabeth; then, uncertain, he stops and listens. A horn call is heard in the distance.

The sound of horns grows fainter in the distance,
And the calls of the huntsmen are lost in the woods . . .
He listens.
All is still! Darkness falls, and on the far horizon
The star of evening casts her beam.
How shall I find the path to the palace again,
Now the mist starts to veil the forest?

Le bruit du cor s'éteint sous l'ombre épaisse,
On entend des chasseurs expirer le refrain . . .

Tout se tait! La nuit vient et la première étoile
Scintille à l'horizon lointain!
Comment vers le palais retrouver mon chemin,
Dans ce bois que la brume voile?

THIBAULT *offstage*

Ola! Come here to me, huntsmen of the King!

Holà! piqueurs! Holà! pages du Roi!

[2] CARLOS - Romance

Je l'ai vue et dans ____ son sou - ri - re,
Io la vi - di e al su - o sor - ri - so
Here I saw her, here ____ I was cap - tured,

38

Fontainebleau! Foresta immensa e solitaria!

Quai giardin, quai rosai, qual Eden di
  splendore
Per Don Carlo potrà questo bosco valer,

Ove Elisabetta sua sorridente apparì?

Lasciai l'Iberia, la corte lasciai,

Di Filippo sfidando il tremendo furore,

Confuso nel corteo del regio ambasciador;

Potei mirarla alfin, la bella fidanzata!

Colei che vidi pria regnar sull'alma mia,

Colei, che per l'amor regnerà sul mio cor!

Io la vidi e al suo sorriso
Scintillar mi parve il sole;
Come l'alma al paradiso
Schiuse a lei la speme, il vol.
Tanta gioia a me prometto
Che s'inebria questo cor;
Dio, sorridi al nostro affetto,
Benedici un casto amor.

Il suon del corno alfin nel bosco tace.

Non più dei cacciator echeggiano i
  clamor.

Cadde il dì! Tace ognun e la stella
  primiera
Scintilla nel lontan spazio azzurrin.
Come del regio ostel rinvenire il cammin?

Questa selva è tanto nera!

Olà! scudier! Olà! paggi del Re!

◇ According to the *Disposizione Scenica*
Don Carlos, Infante of Spain, is 'drawn
this way and that by mixed emotions,
trusting only Rodrigo.'

*Sena Jurinac (Elisabeth) and Eugenio
Fernandi (Don Carlos), Salzburg, 1958
(photo: Salzburger Festspiele)*

39

DON CARLOS

Who is that who is calling through the gloomy forest?

Quelle voix retentit dans la forêt immense?

§

THIBAULT

Ola! Woodcutters, answer my call! To me, to me!

Holà! bons paysans et bûcherons! . . . à moi!

The page appears, with Elisabeth leaning on his arm.

DON CARLOS *retiring to one side*

Ah! A vision enchanting. I see her form approaching.

Ah! Quelle ombre charmante ici vers moi s'avance?

THIBAULT *fearful*

Ah, we have strayed from the path in the dark . . .
May I not take your arm, my lady?
Shadows fall, the night air is cold . . .
We must go on . . .

Ah! J'ai perdu le sentier effacé . . .
Appuyez-vous sur moi, de grâce!
La nuit vient et l'air est glacé . . .
Marchons encor . . .

ELISABETH

Ah! I can go no farther!

Dieu! Comme je suis lasse!

Don Carlos appears and bows to Elisabeth.

THIBAULT *alarmed, to Don Carlos*

Oh! But who is this man?

Ah! Qui donc êtes-vous?

DON CARLOS *to Elisabeth*

A stranger in this land, Come here from Spain . . .

Je suis un étranger . . . Un Espagnol . . .

ELISABETH

Perhaps one of those who accompany The grave Count of Lerma, the ambassador from Spain.

De ceux dont l'escorte accompagne Le vieux comte de Lerme, ambassadeur d'Espagne?

DON CARLOS

Yes, noble lady, and if my arm can serve . . .

Oui noble dame! Et si quelque danger . . . !

THIBAULT *at the back*

Oh, what luck! There in the moonlight, I caught a glimpse of Fontainebleau.
Now let me run straight to the palace, There I can soon summon some help.

O bonheur! Sous la nuit claire, Là-bas j'ai vu Fontainebleau!
Pour ramener votre litière Je vais courir jusqu'au château.

ELISABETH *with authority*

Go, have no fear for me, for am I not betrothed
To Don Carlos, the prince. I trust In the honour of Spain. Thibault, run to the palace . . .

Va, ne crains rien pour moi! Je suis la fiancée
De l'Infant Don Carlos . . . J'ai foi Dans l'honneur espagnol . . . Page, suis ta pensée! . . .

indicating Don Carlos

And this Spaniard will guard the daughter of your King!

Ce seigneur peut garder la fille de ton Roi!

Thibault bows and goes. Don Carlos, his hand on his sword, places himself proudly on Elisabeth's right. Elisabeth raises her eyes to look at Don Carlos; their glances meet and Don Carlos, as if involuntarily, kneels before Elisabeth. He then begins to gather dry branches.

Qual voce risuonò nell'oscura foresta?

§ In the libretto is an additional line: 'L'echo seul lui répond au milieu du silence.'

Olà! venite, boscaioli, a me!

Oh! vision gentile ver me s'avanza!

Non trovo più la via per ritornar . . .

Ecco il mio braccio; sostegno a voi fia.
La notte è buia, il gel vi fa tremar;
Andiam ancor . . .

Ahi! come stanca sono!

Ciel! ma chi sei tu?

Io sono uno stranier,
Uno spagnuol.

Di quei del corteo ch'accompagna
Il signore di Lerma, ambasciator di
Spagna?

Sì, nobil donna! E scudo a voi sarò.

Qual piacer! brillar lontano
Laggiù mirai Fontainebleau.
Per ricondurvi al regio ostello
Sino al castel io correrò.

Va, non temer per me; la regal fidanzata

Di Don Carlo son io; ho fé
Nell'onore spagnuol! Paggio, al castel
t'affretta.

Ei difender saprà la figlia del tuo Re.

*Josephine Barstow as Elisabeth, ENO, 1976
(photo: John Garner)*

41

ELISABETH *astonished*

[3]

But what are you doing?

Que faites-vous donc?

DON CARLOS

On the field,
The soldier learns to make a fire,
Gathering gorse and striking a spark,
From a flint he kindles a flame.
And see how the glittering sparks are
   flying.
Now the flame leaps up in its turn . . .
In battle when the soldier finds the flame
   burns so brightly,
Then he sees it as a sign telling of joy, or
   of love.

A la guerre,
Ayant pour tente le ciel bleu,
Ramassant ainsi la fougère,
On apprend à faire du feu.
Voyez! De ces cailloux a jailli l'étincelle,
Et la flamme brille à son tour!
Au camp, lorsque la flamme est ainsi,
   vive et belle,
Elle annonce, dit-on, la victoire . . . ou
   l'amour!

ELISABETH

Have you come from Madrid?

Vous venez de Madrid?

DON CARLOS

Yes.

Oui.

ELISABETH

And this very evening
Will the peace be signed?

Dès ce soir, peut-être,
On signera la paix . . .

DON CARLOS

Yes, the peace will be signed,
And tonight they'll announce your
   marriage with Don Carlos,
The Infante of Spain.

Oui, sans doute, aujourd'hui,
Vous serez fiancée au fils du Roi, mon
   maître,
A l'Infant Don Carlos!

ELISABETH

Ah, let me hear of him!
This royal stranger, am I wrong to fear
   him?
Far from France I must go!
Will Carlos love his bride?
And in his heart will he wish me to love
   him?

Ah! Parlez-moi de lui!
De l'inconnu j'ai peur malgré moi-même:
Cet hymen, c'est l'exil!
L'Infant m'aimera-t-il?
Et dans son coeur voudra-t-il que je
   l'aime?

DON CARLOS

I know that Carlos will fall at your feet.
His heart is pure, he is worthy of your
   love.

Carlos voudra vous servir à genoux;
Son coeur est pur, il est digne de vous.

ELISABETH

So I must leave my father and this land
   of France.
God's command I obey.

Je vais quitter mon père et la France;

Dieu le veut, j'obéis.

[3] ACT ONE - Duo

Allegro assai moderato

42

Che mai fate voi?

Alla guerra,
Quando il ciel per tenda abbiam,
Sterpi chiedere alla terra
Per la fiamma noi dobbiam!
Già! già! La stipa diè la bramata scintilla,

E la fiamma ecco già brilla.
Al campo, allor che splende così vivace e
bella
La messaggiera ell'è di vittoria . . . o
d'amor.

E lasciaste Madrid?

Sì.

Conchiuder questa sera
La pace si potrà?

Sì, pria del dì novel
Stipular l'imeneo col figlio del mio Re,

Con Don Carlo si dè.

Ah! favelliam di lui!
Ah! terror arcano invade questo core,

Esul lontana andrò,
La Francia lascerò . . .
Ma pari al mio vorrei di lui l'amore.

Carlo vorrà viver al vostro piè,
Arde d'amore; nel vostro core ha fè.

Io lascerò la Francia, e il padre insieme.

Dio lo vuol, partirò;

*Gré Brouwenstijn as Elisabeth in Luchino
Visconti's production, Covent Garden, 1958
(photo: Royal Opera House Archives)*

English	French

To my adopted land
I'll go with joy filled with hope and
  longing!

Dans mon nouveau pays
J'irai joyeuse et pleine d'espérance!

DON CARLOS

And you will find that Carlos loves you
  well.
falling to his knees
Here at your side I can swear he is true!

L'heureux Carlos veut vivre en vous
  aimant:
C'est à vos pieds que j'en fais le serment!

ELISABETH

I am trembling with fear . . . Ah, but
  who can you be?

Tout mon être a frémi! Ciel! Qui donc
  êtes-vous?

DON CARLOS

I am sent by that prince who will claim
  you as bride.

L'envoyé de celui qui sera votre époux.

handing her a locket   §

ELISABETH

What is this?

Cet écrin . . .

DON CARLOS

  It contains a portrait which Don Carlos
Sends to you himself.

    Il contient, madame, le portrait
De votre fiancé.

ELISABETH

    Of Carlos? Can it be true?
I hardly dare . . . Ah, my fears! How I
  tremble!
looking at the portrait and recognising Carlos
Almighty God!

    L'Infant! . . . Il se pourrait! . . .
Je n'ose ouvrir! . . . Ah! J'ai peur de
  moi-même.

O Dieu puissant!

DON CARLOS *falling at her feet*

    Yes, I am Carlos. I love you.

    Je suis Carlos . . . Je t'aime!

ELISABETH *aside*

(With boundless joy so fierce and sweet [4a]
My heart is full!
Ah, you are Carlos, and to my side
Kind Heaven has led you.
I tremble still, but not with fear. [4b]
Still I tremble!
And you're my Carlos! Oh, my beloved,
You have my heart!)

(De quels transports poignants et doux
Mon âme est pleine!
Ah! C'est Carlos, à mes genoux
Un dieu l'amène! §§
Ah! Je tremblais et de bonheur
Encor je tremble!
Oui, c'est Carlos! A sa voix semble
S'ouvrir mon coeur!)

DON CARLOS

My love is true and God himself
Has led me here. God led me here.

Ah! Je vous aime, et Dieu lui-même
A vos genoux, Dieu m'a conduit!

ELISABETH

If His hand led you here in this enchanted
night,

Si sa main nous guida dans cette étrange
nuit,

[4a] ELISABETH, *to herself*

Allegro giusto
dolcissimo Cant. espr.

De quels trans - ports ___ poig - nants et doux mon â - me est plei - ne!
Di qual a - mor ___ di quan - t'ar - dor que - st'al - maè pie - na!
With bound - less joy ___ so fierce and sweet my heart __ is filled!

Un'altra patria avrò.
Ne andrò giuliva, e pieno il cor di speme.

E Carlo pur amandovi vivirà;

Al vostro piè lo giuro, ei v'amera.

Perché mi balza il cor? Ciel! chi siete
mai?

Del prence messagger, per voi questo
recai.

§ Voici mes lettres de créance
Près la fille du Roi de France.

Un suo don!

            V'inviò l'immagin sua fedel,
Noto vi fia così.

         Gran Dio! . . . Io lo vedrò! . . .
Non oso aprir! . . . Ah! ma pur vederlo
bramo.

Possente Iddio!

         Carlo son io . . . e t'amo!

(Di qual amor, di quant'ardor
Quest'alma è piena!
Al suo destin voler divin
Or m'incatena!
Arcan terror m'avea nel cor,
E ancor ne tremo . . .
Amata io son, gaudio supremo
Ne sento in cor!)

§§ C'est don Carlos, qu'à mes genoux
L'amour amène.

Sì, t'amo, t'amo, te sola io bramo,
Vivrò per te, per te morrò!

Se l'amor ci guidò, se a me t'avvicinò,

[4b]

più mosso

Ah! je   trem - blais — et —— de   bon - heur — en - cor   je
Ar - can   ter - ror —— m'a - vea   nel   cor, —— e   an - cor   ne
I   trem - ble   still — but — not   with   fear, — ah, — still   I

Then He intends I should love you.
a cannon shot
Do you hear?

Ah! C'est qu'il veut aussi que je vous aime!

Ecoutez!

DON CARLOS

Yes, the cannon rings out!

Le canon retentit.

ELISABETH

Happy day.
A sign that the Court's rejoicing.

Jour heureux!
C'est un signal de fête.

The terraces of Fontainebleau, illuminated, shine in the distance.

DON CARLOS AND ELISABETH

Oh, God be praised! Then peace is with us!

Dieu soit loué! La paix est faite!

ELISABETH

Over there! See the palace is blazing with light.

Regardez! Le palais étincelle de feux!

DON CARLOS

Bare frozen boughs and leafless branches
To my marvelling eyes you adorn with
fragrant flowers.

Bois dépouillés, ravins, broussailles,
A mes yeux enchantés, vous vous couvrez
de fleurs!

ELISABETH

Ah!

Ah!

DON CARLOS AND ELISABETH

Now in the sight of God, let us unite our hearts
In this embrace of our betrothal!

Sous les regards de Dieu, unissons nos deux
coeurs
Dans le baiser des fiançailles!

DON CARLOS

Ah, no trembling now, for you are mine.
You are now my bride.
No trembling now, but raise your eyes.
See your Carlos beside you.

Ah! Ne tremble pas, reviens à toi.
Ma belle fiancée:
Ne tremble pas, lève sur moi
Ta paupière baissée.

ELISABETH

Ah, I tremble still, but not with fear.
With joy my heart is full.
And joy overwhelms my fainting soul.
It is joy makes me tremble.

Ah! Je tremble encor, mais non d'effroi.
Lisez dans ma pensée:
Et ce bonheur nouveau pour moi
Tient mon âme oppressée.

DON CARLOS AND ELISABETH

We'll live united, joined by vows,
Those vows that long have bound us,
And all our life we'll live
United by our love.

Toujours unis par le serment
Qui dès longtemps nous lie:
Marchons tous deux dans cette vie
En nous aimant!

Scena and Finale.

*Thibault enters with pages bearing torches. The pages halt at the back of the stage, and Thibault alone
advances to Elisabeth.*

THIBAULT *kneeling and kissing Elisabeth's dress*

To this page kneeling before you,
To this page bearing news of joy,
Will you grant him the favour that he now
will ask you?
Ah, may I ever serve at your side?

A celui qui vous vient, Madame,
Apporter un message heureux
Accordez la faveur que de vous il réclame,

Celle de ne jamais vous quitter!

ELISABETH *raising him*

But of course!

Je le veux!

46

Il fe' perché ci vuol felici appieno.

Qual rumor!

Il cannone echeggiò.

Fausto dì!
Questo è segnal di festa!

Sì, lode al ciel! La pace è stretta!

Qual baglior? È il castel che risplende
    così.

Sparì l'orror della foresta;
Tutto è gioia, splendor, tutto è delizia, amor!

Ah!

Il ciel ci vegga alfin uniti cor a cor

Nell'imeneo che Dio ci appresta!

Ah! non temer, ritorna in te,
O bella fidanzata!
Angel d'amor, leva su me
La tua pupilla amata.

Ah! Se tremo ancor terror non è,
Mi sento già rinata!
A voluttà nuova per me
È l'alma abbandonata.

Rinnovelliam, ebbri d'amor,
Il giuro che ci univa;
Lo disse il labbro, il ciel l'udiva,
Lo fece il cor!

Al fedel ch'ora viene, o signora,
Un messaggio felice a recar,
Accordate un favor; di serbarmi con voi

Nè mai lasciarvi più.

Sia pur!

*Joan Hammond (Elisabeth) and James
Johnston (Don Carlos), Sadler's Wells,
1951; producer, George Devine, designer
Roger Furse (photo: ENO Archive)*

THIBAULT

I hail you Queen of Spain, King Philip's royal bride.	Salut, ô Reine, épouse de Philippe deux! §

ELISABETH *trembling*

Ah, no! For to his son, to Don Carlos, I'm plighted!	Non! C'est à l'Infant que je suis destinée!

THIBAULT

On the King of Spain himself your father has bestowed you.	Au roi Philippe deux Henri vous à donnée!
Yes, you are Queen now!	Vous êtes reine!

ELISABETH

Oh God!	O ciel!

DON CARLOS

Now, in sudden fear, I see the dread abyss, and my soul is afraid!	Muet, glacé d'horreur, Devant l'abîme ouvert je frémis de terreur!

ELISABETH

Death to my dream of delight then. No, it is braver to fight When the fates prove unkind and cruel. Nobler far, I shall refuse him! Why should I bear chains of sadness? I would rather go to my grave!	L'heure fatale est sonnée! Non! Contre la destinée Combattre est vaillant et beau. Oui, plutôt que d'être reine Et de porter cette chaîne, Je veux descendre au tombeau!

DON CARLOS

Death to my dream of delight then. Destiny cruel and ruthless Shatters my dream of delight. Ah, I shall die, grief overwhelms me. Now I shall bear chains of sadness, Until I go to my grave!	L'heure fatale est sonnée! La cruelle destinée Brise ce rêve si beau! Et de regrets mon âme est pleine, Nous traînerons notre chaîne Jusqu'à la paix du tombeau.

Remainder of the Finale.

The above, the Count of Lerma, the Spanish ambassador, the Countess of Aremberg, ladies-in-waiting to Elisabeth, pages, attendants bearing torches and a litter, the people.

CHORUS

Songs of rejoicing, songs of rejoicing, Bravely and clearly, Your voices raise. Peace is returning, sing of your gladness. End all your sadness, In hymns of praise. Blessings and joy, praise to our lady. Thanks to her beauty, Peace comes again. Now we hail her as we come to meet her. Gladly we greet her, As Queen of Spain.	O chants de fête et d'allégresse, Frappez sans cesse Les airs joyeux, La paix heureuse est ramenée Par l'hyménée, Du haut des cieux! Salut et joie à la plus belle, Honneur à celle Qui va demain, Sur un trône où Dieu l'accompagne, Au Roi d'Espagne Donner sa main!

ELISABETH

Then it is true!	C'en est donc fait!

DON CARLOS

The fates conspire against us.	Fatales destinées.

ELISABETH

To grief they have condemned us.	Nos âmes condamnées . . .

48

Regina, vi saluto, sposa a Filippo Re.

No! sono all'Infante dal padre fidanzata.

§The libretto has the following instead:
Que le bonheur en tous lieux
accompagne
Celle qui va monter sur le trône
d'Éspagne
Aux côtés de Philippe deux!

Al monarca spagnuol v'ha Enrico destinata.

Siete Regina.

Ahimè!

Nel cor mi corse un gel!
L'abisso s'apre a me! E tu lo soffri, o ciel!

L'ora fatale è suonata!
Contro la sorte spietata
Crudo fia meno il pugnar.
L'ora fatal è già suonata!
Per sottrarmi a tanta pena,
Per fuggir la ria catena,
Fin la morte io vo' sfidar!

L'ora fatale è suonata!
M'era la vita beata,
Cruda, funesta ora m'appar.
Di dolor quest'alma è piena,
Ah! dovrò la mia catena
In eterno trascinar!

Inni di festa lieti echeggiate,
E salutate
Il lieto dì.
La pace appresta felici istanti;
Due cori amanti
Il cielo unì!
Gloria ed onor alla più bella,
Onor a quella
Che de' doman
Assisa in soglio, gentil compagna,
Al Re di Spagna
Dar la sua man!

Tutto sparve . . .

Sorte ingrata!

Al dolor son condannata!

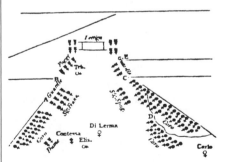

Diagram from the 'Disposizione Scenica':
On the last bars of the Chorus, there enter
from E:
1. 4 pages with torches
2. The Count of Lerma, taking the
Countess of Aremberg's arm
3. 2 Ladies-in-waiting
4. 4 French nobles
5. 4 Spanish nobles
6. A litter carried by 8 pages
7. 7 guards of the French king

49

DON CARLOS AND ELISABETH

My life can hold no joy.	Ne connaîtront jamais
Alas, no contentment or peace!	Le bonheur ni la paix!

ELISABETH

Ah!	Ah!

DON CARLOS

Alas! Alas! All's at an end.	C'en est donc fait!
To grief they have condemned us.	A d'éternels regrets nos âmes
	condamnées ...

THE COUNT OF LERMA *to Elisabeth*

His Majesty King Henry of France, your noble father,	Le très-glorieux Roi de France, votre père,
To the ruler of Spain and the Indies promises	Au puissant Roi d'Espagne et de l'Inde a promis
The hand of his fair, noble daughter.	La main de sa fille bien chère.
At this price now the long cruel warfare can cease.	Une guerre cruelle est finie à ce prix. §
But King Philip decrees you alone must decide it.	Mais Philippe ne veut vous devoir qu'à vous-même,
Will you accept the hand of this monarch who loves you?	Acceptez-vous la main de ce roi qui vous aime?

CHORUS OF WOMEN

O Princess, please accept King Philip as your lord!	O Princesse, acceptez Philippe pour époux!
Bring peace! We've suffered long, take pity on our fate.	La paix! Nous souffrons tant, ayez pitié de nous!

THE COUNT OF LERMA

What do you answer?	Votre réponse?

ELISABETH *with a dying voice*

Yes.	Oui!

CHORUS

Ah, God has heard us,	Dieu nous entende,
O noble heart ...	O vaillant coeur!
O may He grant you	Et qu'il vous rende
Joy and delight!	Notre bonheur!

DON CARLOS AND ELISABETH

(I must suffer in silence.	(C'est l'angoisse suprême!
I shall die of grief. Ah!	Je me sens mourir! Ah!
All my life's at an end. O my grief and regret!)	C'en est fait! O douleurs! O regrets!)

CHORUS

Gladly we hail you, Queen of Spain!	Reine d'Espagne, gloire à vous!

Elisabeth, led by the Count of Lerma, mounts her litter. Don Carlos remains in despair, his head in his hands, on the rock where Elisabeth was seated. The procession moves off.

DON CARLOS *in despair*

Alas! Alas!	Hélas! Hélas!
Grief overwhelms me,	L'heure fatale est sonnée,
Fate is cruel.	La cruelle destinée
Destiny cruel and ruthless shatters my dream of delight.	Brise mon rêve si beau!
I shall die of grief, I shall die of grief!	O destin fatal, ô destin fatal!

Spariva il sogno d'or!
Svaniva dal mio cor!

Ah!

Tutto finì! Al più crudel dolor
Nostr'alma è condannata! Tanto amor ora
finì.

Il glorioso Re di Francia, il grande Enrico,

Al monarca di Spagna e dell'India vuol dar

La man d'Elisabetta sua figliuola.
Questo vincol sarà suggello d'amistà.

Ma Filippo lasciarvi libertade vuol intera;

Gradite voi la man del mio Re . . . che la
spera?

Principessa, accettate la man che v'offre il
Re:
Pietà! La pace avrem alfin! pietà di noi!

Che rispondete?

Sì.

Vi benedica
Iddio dal ciel!
La sorte amica
Vi sia fedel!

(È l'angoscia suprema!
Mi sento morir! Ah!
O martir! o dolor! Non v'ha duol più
crudel!)

Regina Ispana, gloria, onor!

Ahimè! Ahimè!
L'ora fatale è suonata!
M'era la vita beata,
Cruda, funesta or m'appar. Sparì un sogno
così bel!
O destin fatal, o destin crudel!

§ The libretto gives the line as:
'Après une trop longue guerre,'
with an additional line thereafter:
'Ce lieu scellera leur serment d'être amis;'

*Plácido Domingo as Don Carlos,
Metropolitan Opera, 1971 (photo:
Metropolitan Opera Archive)*

Act Two *

Scene One. *The cloister of the San Yuste monastery. Right, an illuminated chapel, with the tomb of Charles V visible through gilded grilles: left, a door leading to the outside; at the back a garden with large cypress trees. It is dawn.* ◊

Scena and Prayer. [5]

A choir of monks is chanting in the chapel. Onstage, a kneeling monk prays before the tomb.

CHOIR OF MONKS

Charles the Fifth, our mighty Lord,
Lies here in dust and lifeless clay;
While his immortal soul in anguish prays
For peace and mercy on high.

[6] Charles-Quint, l'auguste Empereur,
N'est plus que cendre et que poussière.
Et maintenant, son âme altière
Est tremblante aux pieds du Seigneur!

THE MONK

All the earth he claimed as his kingdom;
He forgot that king set on high,
Who rules both the earth and the sky.
Though his pride grew so great, greater
    yet was his fall.

Il voulait régner sur le monde,
Oubliant celui dont la main
Aux astres montra leur chemin.
Son orgueil était grand, sa démence
    profonde!

CHOIR OF MONKS

May the lightning flash of your anger
Turn to pardon for him, O Lord.

Que les traits de votre colère
Se détournent de lui, Seigneur!

THE MONK

But God is great! With fiery glances
He can shake the earth and the sky!
Ah! God who forgives all who repent,
To whom none turns in vain,
God, show mercy, grant him pardon and
    peace.

Dieu seul est grand! Ses traits de flamme
Font trembler la terre et les cieux!
Ah! Maître miséricordieux,
Penché vers le pécheur, accordez à son âme
La paix et le pardon, qui descendent des
    cieux. §

CHOIR OF MONKS

Oh, Lord, the flash of your anger
Turn to pardon for him.

Seigneur, que votre colère §§
Se détourne de lui.

*A bell tolls. The monks come out of the chapel, cross the stage and go out. Don Carlos appears beneath the vaults of the cloister.***

DON CARLOS

In the cloister of San Yuste, where Charles
    the Fifth,
My father's mighty sire, once came to end
    his life,
I seek in vain for peace, to forget all the
    past.
But she was cruelly taken from me;
Her image haunts me still in this quiet
    house of God.

Au couvent de Saint-Just, où termina sa
    vie
Mon aïeul Charles-Quint, de sa grandeur
    lassé,
Je cherche en vain la paix et l'oubli du
    passé:
De celle qui me fut ravie
L'image erre avec moi dans ce cloître
    glacé!

[5] SCENA AND PRAYER

* The four-act Milan version begins here.

◊ The diagram from the *Disposizione Scenica* for this act is the same as Act Five on page 135.

Carlo il sommo Imperatore
Non è più che muta polve!
Del celeste suo fattore
L'alma altera or trema al piè.

Ei voleva regnare sul mondo,
Obliando Colui che nel ciel
Segna agli astri il cammino fedel.
L'orgoglio immenso fu, fu l'error suo
  profondo!

Del celeste suo fattore
L'alma altera or trema al piè.

Grande è Dio sol, e s'Ei lo vuole
Fa tremar la terra ed il ciel!
Ah! Misericorde Iddio,
Pietoso al peccator, allo spirto addolorato
Dà la requie ed il perdon che discendono dal
  ciel.

§ La paix et le pardon que de vous il
réclame!

§§ En votre clémence il espère,
Ayez pitié de lui, Seigneur!'

Signor, il tuo furor non piombi,
Non piombi sul suo cor.

†

** According to the libretto, 'Day dawns slowly. Carlos, pale and haggard, appears wandering beneath the vaults of the cloister. He stops to listen.'

Al chiostro di San Giusto ove finì la vita

L'avo mio Carlo Quinto, stanco di gloria
  e onor,
La pace cerco invan, che tanto ambisce il
  cor!
Di lei che m'han rapita
L'immago erra con me del chiostro
  nell'orror!

† Because it does not include the opening 'Fontainebleau' act, the four-act Milan version here introduces an aria for Don Carlos, 'Io l'ho perduta', a reworking of his romance in Act One of the five-act versions (see appendix). It replaces the next five lines.

The Milan version differs from this point until the Carlos/Rodrigo duet on p. 59 (see appendix).

[6] CHOIR OF MONKS, *chanting in the chapel*

Andante sostenuto assai

Char - les -Quint, l'au - guste Em - pe - reur,   n'est plus que cen - dre et que pous - siè - re.
Car - lo, il som - mo Im - pe - ra - to-re,   non   è   più che mu - ta   pol-ve.
Charles the fifth, our migh - ty   Lord,   lies here in dust and life - less clay.

THE MONK *who has risen, approaching Don Carlos*

My son, all the griefs that assail us
Must still be endured in this place.
The peace that your heart so yearns for
Will be found at the throne of grace!

Mon fils, les douleurs de la terre
Nous suivent encor en ce lieu.
La paix que votre cœur espère
Ne se trouve qu'auprès de Dieu!

He continues on his way.

DON CARLOS

Oh my God, how I tremble!
For I thought that I heard
The voice of mighty Charles!
Does he hide his regal presence
Beneath a humble robe?
For here they say the Emperor still is seen.

A cette voix, je frissonne!
J'ai cru voir . . . ô terreur!
L'ombre de l'Empereur!
Sous le froc cachant sa couronne
Et sa cuirasse d'or;
Ici, dit-on, il apparaît encor!

THE MONK *growing ever more distant*

That peace will be found at the throne of
God.

La paix ne se trouve qu'auprès de Dieu.

DON CARLOS

How that voice makes me tremble!
I'm afraid! I'm afraid!

Cette voix! Je frissonne . . .
O terreur! O terreur!

Scena and Duet. *

RODRIGO ◊ *brought in by a lay brother*

There he is, there's the Prince!

Le voilà! C'est l'Infant!

DON CARLOS *about to throw himself into his arms*

      Oh, my Rodrigo!

      O mon Rodrigue!

RODRIGO *stopping him with a gesture*

I am here to seek an audience with the
Infante of Spain!

Je demande audience au noble fils du roi!

DON CARLOS *coldly*

I grant your request, Marquis of Posa!

Soyez le bienvenu, Marquis de Posa!

At a sign from Don Carlos, the lay brother retires.
throwing himself into Rodrigo's arms

      You!

      Toi!

My Rodrigo, how gladly to my heart I press
you!
To me, oppressed by grief,
God sends you here, angel bringing me
comfort!

Mon Rodrigue! C'est toi que dans mes bras
je presse!
Vers moi, dans ma douleur,
Dieu te conduit, ange consolateur!

RODRIGO

Ah, my Carlos, oh my friend!
I come from Flanders, where I served
in the army.
I come to intercede before the prince
of Spain,
For that brave and noble people whose
blood flows in streams!
You alone can help and save them!
In despair and in anguish, see a race on
their knees,
A suffering race of martyrs, seeking
a saviour in you.
But what is this? Why do you grow so pale?

Ah, cher Prince, mon Carlos! †
J'étais en Flandre, où je suivais l'armée!
Je viens intercéder près de l'Infant Carlos
Pour ce noble pays où le sang coule
à flots!
Secourez la Flandre opprimée!
Dans le deuil et l'effroi tout un peuple
à genoux,
Un peuple de martyrs, lève les bras
vers vous!
Mais qu'ai-je vu? Quelle pâleur mortelle!

Il duolo della terra
Nel chiostro ancor c'insegue;
Del core sol la guerra
In ciel si calmerà.

La sua voce! Il cor mi trema!
Mi pareva . . . qual terror!
Veder l'Imperator
Che nelle lane il serto asconde
E la lorica d'ôr.
È voce che nel chiostro appaia ancor!

Del core la guerra in ciel si calmerà.

Questa voce! Il cor trema . . .
O terror! O terror!

Egli è quì; Carlo mio!

O mio Rodrigo!

Brevi istanti domando al figlio del
   mio Re!

* From this point until the end of the
opera, the four-act Milan version and
the five-act Modena version of 1886
follow the same course.

◊ According to the *Disposizione Scenica*,
Rodrigo, Marquis of Posa, is
'enthusiastic, straightforward, loyal,
representing the ideals of liberty and
patriotism.'

Concessi sono a voi, nobil signor di Posa!

                                          Oh!
Mio Rodrigo, sei tu che sul mio core io
   stringo!
Ver me, nel mio dolore,
Dio ti conduce, angel consolatore!

O mio prence, amato Carlo!
Qui dalle Fiandre ove seguii l'armata,

Io vengo a supplicar l'Infante mio Signor

Per quel nobil paese dissanguato
   dall'oppressor!
Soccorrete le Fiandre oppresse!
Nel terrore e nel duol tutto un popol
   prostrato,
Un popol torturato tende le braccia a voi!

Ma che vid'io! quale pallor, qual pena!

† This speech was cut before the Paris
première in 1867, and a shortened text
substituted. It is absent also, therefore,
from the Milan and Modena versions.

Why this flash of despair that I see in your
glances?
And not a word!... You only sigh!...
You weep!
Dearest Carlos, let me share your grief
and calm your pain!

Un éclair douloureux dans vos yeux
étincelle!
Vous vous taisez... vous soupirez...
des pleurs!...
Mon Carlos, donne-moi ma part de tes
douleurs!

DON CARLOS

Ah, my comrade, my friend, my brother,
Let me weep in your arms!
In all my father's empire
I have only this heart! Do not banish me
from it!

Mon compagnon, mon ami, mon frère,
Laisse-moi pleurer dans tes bras.
Dans tout l'empire de mon père,
Je n'ai que ce coeur! Ne m'en bannis pas!

RODRIGO

In the name of dear friendship,
Of days past, of happy days,
Open your heart to me!

Au nom d'une amitié chère,
Des jours passés, des jours heureux!
Ouvre-moi ton coeur!

DON CARLOS

Shall I tell?
Then learn all my sorrow!
Yes, learn what fearful blow fate has
struck in my heart!
I love, with a passionate fire,
Elisabeth!

Tu le veux?
Eh bien, donc, connais ma misère!
Frémis du trait fatal dont mon coeur est
blessé!
J'aime d'un amour insensé
Elisabeth...

RODRIGO

Your mother!
God in Heaven!

Ta mère!
Dieu puissant!

DON CARLOS

Yes, I know... you're unable to look
In my eyes... then I'm lost! My Rodrigo
forsakes me.
Rodrigo turns away and renounces his
friend!

Tu pâlis! Ton regard, malgré toi,
Fuit le mien! Malheureux! Mon Rodrigue,
lui-même,
Rodrigue, avec horreur, se détourne de
moi!

RODRIGO

Your Rodrigo loves you!
And I swear by my faith,
You suffer... that is all in the world that
I see!

Non, Carlos, ton Rodrigue t'aime!
Par ma foi de chrétien,
Tu souffres... A mes yeux, l'univers n'est
plus rien!

DON CARLOS

My comrade, my friend, my brother,
Let me weep in your arms!
In all my father's empire
I have only this heart! Do not banish me
from it!

Ah! Mon compagnon, mon ami, mon frère,
Laisse-moi pleurer dans tes bras!
Dans tout l'empire de mon père,
Je n'ai que ce coeur, ne m'en bannis pas!

RODRIGO

O Carlos, my friend, my brother,
Again I open to you my heart!
For your father's golden sceptre
My heart would not change!
Has your secret been discovered by the
King?

Oh Carlos, mon ami, mon frère,
Je t'ouvre encor mon coeur!
Pour le sceptre d'or de ton père,
Mon coeur, ne changerait pas!
Ton secret par le Roi s'est-il laissé
surprendre?

DON CARLOS

No!

Non!

Un lampo di dolor sul ciglio tuo balena!

Muto sei tu!... sospiri!... hai tristo
   il cor!...
Carlo mio, con me, dividi il tuo pianto, il
   tuo dolor.

Mio fedel, fratel d'affetto,
Fa ch'io pianga sul tuo sen.
Nell'impero al Re soggetto,
Il tuo core, trovo almen!

Dell'amicizia in nome,
Ed in memoria ai lieti giorni!
M'apri il tuo cor!

               Tu lo vuoi?
Ebben sia, ti svelo il segreto!
Nel cor acuto stral lasciò piaga mortal!

Amo d'ardente amor
Elisabetta...

               Tua madre!
Giusto ciel!

               Qual pallor! Lo sguardo,
Chini al suol! Oh tristo me! Tu stesso,

Mio Rodrigo, t'allontani da me!

*Robert Merrill (Rodrigo) and Jussi Björling
(Don Carlos), 1950 (photo: Metropolitan
Opera Archive)*

No, mio Carlo, Rodrigo ancor t'ama!
Lo posso a Dio giurar,
Tu soffri! Già per me l'universo dispar!

Ah! Mon fedel, fratel d'affetto
Fa ch'io pianga sul tuo sen!
Nell'impero al Re soggetto,
Il tuo core io trovi almen!

Carlo mio, fratel d'affetto,
Piangi sul mio sen!
Nell'impero al Re soggetto,
Tu trovasti un core almen!
Questo arcano dal Re non fu sorpreso
   ancora?

No!

RODRIGO

You must ask his leave to depart now for Flanders.	Obtiens donc de lui de partir pour la Flandre.
Thus by a deed worthy of you,	Par un effort digne de toi
Conquer your heart ... and you shall learn there,	Brise ton coeur ... et viens apprendre,
Among those suffering people how a king should rule!	Parmi des malheureux, ton dur métier de Roi!

DON CARLOS

That brave advice I'll follow!	Je te suivrai, mon frère!

A bell tolls, monks cross the stage.

RODRIGO

But listen!	Ecoute!
The cloister doors will soon be unbarred, admitting	Les portes du couvent vont s'ouvrir! C'est sans doute
Your father and also the Queen.	Philippe avec la Reine!

DON CARLOS

Elisabeth!	Elisabeth!

RODRIGO

O Carlos,	Carlos,
At my side show resolve and rouse your fainting spirits!	Près de moi, fortifie une âme qui chancelle!
For there in Flanders the people wait to greet their saviour.	Ta destinée encor peut être utile et belle ...
We'll pray to God to fire your soul with strength!	Demande à Dieu la force d'un héros!

DON CARLOS AND RODRIGO

God, who has brought us together,	[7] Dieu, tu semas dans nos âmes
Fire our hearts with flames of glory,	Un rayon des mêmes flammes,
Fire that is noble and pure,	Le même amour exalté,
Fire of love that will set men free!	L'amour de la liberté!
God, grant that this love may fire us,	Dieu, qui de nos coeurs sincères
May freedom call and inspire us!	As fait les coeurs de deux frères,
Accept the vow that we swear!	Accepte notre serment!
We shall die united in love!	Nous mourrons en nous aimant!

Philip appears, leading Elisabeth, preceded by the monks.

RODRIGO

They are here!	Les voilà!

DON CARLOS

I'm afraid! When I see her I tremble!	Je frémis! Je meurs à sa vue!

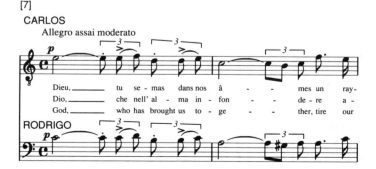

58

Ottien dunque da lui di partir per la Fiandra.

Taccia il tuo cor, degna di te
Opra farai; apprendi omai

In mezzo a gente oppressa a divenir un
Re!

Ti seguirò, fratello.

Ascolta!
Veggo che il santo asil s'apre già.

Qui verran Filippo e la Regina!

Elisabetta!

Accanto
A me rinfranca l'alma all'onor rubella,

Può la tua sorte ancor esser felice e bella!

Domanda a Dio che infonda in te vigor!

†

Dio, che nell'alma infondere
Amor volesti e speme
Desio nel cor accendere
Tu dêi di libertà;
Giuriamo insiem di vivere
E di morire insieme;
In terra, in ciel congiungere
Ci può la tua bontà.

Vengon già!

Oh terror! Al sol vederla io tremo!

Ettore Bastianini as Rodrigo, Metropolitan Opera, 1954 (photo: Metropolitan Opera Archive)

† The end of the section revised in the Milan version (see note † on page 53, and the appendix).

CARLOS

-on ____ des ___ mê - mes ___ flam - - mes, ____
-mor ____ vo - le - sti e - spe - - - me, ____
hearts ____ with _ flames of ___ glo - - - - ry

RODRIGO

RODRIGO

Be brave!   Courage!

Rodrigo has stepped aside from Don Carlos, who bows beneath Philip's suspicious glance and strives to master his emotion. Elisabeth starts on seeing Don Carlos. The King and Queen go to the chapel.

DON CARLOS

She is his wife, and I have lost her!   Elle est à lui, grand Dieu! Je l'ai perdue!

RODRIGO

Stay by my side, be strong and steel your   Viens, près de moi ton coeur sera plus
heart!   fort!

DON CARLOS AND RODRIGO

We'll live as one and together we'll die!   Soyons unis pour la vie et la mort!
God, accept the vow that we swear!   Dieu accepte notre serment
Let us live and die united in love,   De mourir en nous aimant!
Living as one, bound together in death.   Soyons unis pour la vie et la mort!

Scene Two. *A delightful spot outside the San Yuste monastery gates. A fountain, grassy banks, clusters of orange trees, pines and lentisks; the blue mountains of Estremadura on the horizon; at the back, on the left, the monastery gate, with steps leading up to it. The ladies-in-waiting are seated on the grass and around the fountain. A page is tuning a guitar.*

Chorus of Ladies and the Veil Song.

LADIES-IN-WAITING

Where the pine grove is green and shady   Sous ces bois au feuillage immense,
Where the soft grasssy banks invite us,   D'un rempart d'ombre et de silence
By this cloister we may not enter,   Entourant la maison de Dieu,
We have found a secure retreat.   Sous ces pins, dont l'abri nous tente,
In this glade where the trees delight us,   On peut fuir la chaleur ardente
We'll escape from the sun's fierce heat.   Et l'éclat de ce ciel en feu!

Thibault enters with Eboli.

THIBAULT

The fountain cools the heat of summer,   Les fleurs ici couvrent la terre,
The cypress make a shade above,   Les pins ouvrent leurs parasols,
And when at evening shadows lengthen,   Et sous l'ombrage pour vous plaire,
The nightingales will sing of love.   Vont s'éveiller les rossignols.

THIBAULT, LADIES-IN-WAITING

Here the shady cypress invite us,   Qu'il fait bon, assis sous les arbres,
And the murmuring fountain will   Ecouter bruir sur les marbres
  charm us,
For its song is a sigh of love!   La chanson de la source en pleurs!
To make the weary hours pass fleetly,   Qu'il fait bon, à l'heure brûlante,
We'll rest sweetly,   Charmer du jour la marche lente
While fierce sunlight blazes up above.   Parmi l'ombre et parmi les fleurs!

EBOLI ◊

And since within these walls no woman   Puisque dans ce couvent la Reine des
  may enter,   Espagnes
Except the Queen of Spain, shall we try,   Peut seule entrer; voulez-vous, mes
  dear companions,   compagnes,
To while away the time with some sport,   Chercher en attendant que le ciel ait pâli,
  or some play?
Perhaps a song . . . what would best divert   Quelque jeu qui nous divertisse?
  us?

THIBAULT, LADIES-IN-WAITING

But you must choose and we shall follow,   Nous suivrons tous votre caprice,
O charming Princess Eboli!   Charmante Princesse Eboli!

60

Coraggio!

Ei la fe' sua! Io l'ho perduta!

Vien presso a me, il tuo cor più forte
   avrai!

Vivremo insiem e morremo insiem!
Sarà l'estremo anelito,
Sarà un grido: Libertà!
Vivremo insiem! Morremo insiem!

Sotto ai folti, immensi abeti,
Che fan d'ombre e di quieti
Mite schermo al sacro ostel,
Ripariamo e a noi ristori
Dien i rezzi ai vivi ardori,
Che su noi dardeggia il ciel!

Di mille fior si copre il suolo,
Dei pini s'ode il sussurrar,
E sotto l'ombra aprir il vol
Qui l'usignuol più lieto par.

Bello è udire in fra le piante
Mormorar la fonte amante,

Stilla a stilla i suoi dolor!
E se il sole è più cocente,
Le ore far del dì men lente
In fra l'ombra e in mezzo ai fior!

Tra queste mura pie la Regina di Spagna

Può sola penetrar. Volete voi, mie
   compagne,
Già che le stelle in ciel spuntate ancor
   non son,
Cantar qualche canzon?

Seguir vogliam il tuo capriccio;
O principessa, attente udrem.

*Diagram of this moment in the 'Disposizione
Scenica'.*
'Philip enters from B, giving Elisabeth his
hand. 2 pages follow, each carrying a prayer
book on a velvet cushion: after them come
the Count of Lerma, 2 ladies-in-waiting of
the Queen, 4 Spanish nobles and 4 monks.'
[C indicates the tomb of Charles V.]

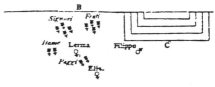

◊ According to the *Disposizione Scenica*
Princess Eboli is 'very elegant, frivolous,
capricious, easily excited.'

61

EBOLI *to Thibault*

Come, my friend, strike up your mandoline,	Apportez une mandoline,
And together we'll sing,	Et chantons tour à tour,
The song of the Saracen maiden,	Chantons la chanson sarrasine,
Known as the Veil song.	Celle du voile indulgent à l'amour!

EBOLI, THIBAULT AND LADIES-IN-WAITING

Let's sing!	Chantons!

EBOLI

In the marble palace	[8] Au palais des fées,
Of the Moorish king,	Des rois grenadins,
Where the flowers bloom sweetly,	Devant les nymphées
Where the fountains sing,	De ces beaux jardins,
A lovely veiled maiden	Couverte d'un voile
Came to walk one night,	Une femme, un soir,
Sat beside the fountain	A la belle étoile
In the star's dim light.	Seule vint s'asseoir.
And Achmet, who was king	Achmet, le roi maure,
In those days, passed by,	En passant la vit,
And that veiled beauty	Et voilée encore,
Attracted his eye.	Elle le ravit.
'Come, my pretty maiden,	'Viens, ma souveraine,
Come rule in my life',	Régner à ma cour,'
He declared . . . and said	Lui dit-il: 'la Reine
He was bored with his wife.	N'a plus mon amour.'

EBOLI, THIBAULT AND LADIES-IN-WAITING

Ah! O pretty maidens, look to your veils!	Ah! O jeunes filles, tissez des voiles!
Weave them by sunlight, wear them by night.	Quand le ciel brille des feux du jour,
Then, when the moon shines bright up above,	Aux lueurs des étoiles,
You may capture	Les voiles
The man that you love!	Sont chers à l'amour!

EBOLI

'I can scarcely see you,	'J'entrevois à peine,
In this shady park.	Dans l'obscur jardin,
Dainty feet and fingers	Tes cheveux d'ébène,
Glimmer through the dark.	Ton pied enfantin.
The King now desires	O fille charmante!
To make your heart his own.	Un roi t'aimera:
Be the foremost, fairest flower	Sois la fleur vivante
Around my throne!	De mon Alhambra.

[8] EBOLI The Veil Song

A me recate la mandolina:
E cantiam tutte insiem,
Cantiam la canzon saracina,
Quella del velo, propizia all'amor.

Cantiam!

Nei giardin del bello
Saracin ostello,
All'olezzo, al rezzo
Degli allôr, dei fior
Una bell'almea,
Tutta chiusa in vel,
Contemplar parea
Una stella in ciel.
Mohammed, Re moro,
Al giardin sen va
Dice a lei: 'T'adoro,
O gentil beltà!
Vien, a sé t'invita
Per regnare il Re;
La Regina ambita
Non è più da me.'

Ah! Tessete i veli, vaghe donzelle,
Mentre è nei cieli l'astro maggior,
Ché sono i veli,
Al brillar delle stelle
Più cari all'amor.

'Ma discerno appena —
Chiaro il ciel non è —
I capelli belli,
La man breve, il piè.
Deh! solleva il velo
Che t'asconde a me;
Esser come il cielo
Senza vel tu de'?

*Diagram of Act Two, scene two, in the
'Disposizione Scenica': 1. Backcloth at the
rear representing the mountains of
Estremadura; 2. indented curtain; E
monastery; D steps of a path leading to the
doors of the monastery; F fountain.*

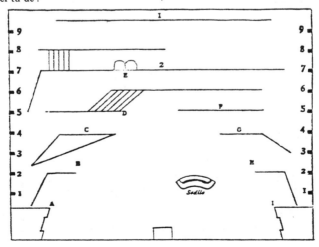

But take off that veil	Mais quitte ce voile,
In response to my love.	Bel astre charmant,
Shine bright and unveiled	Fais comme l'étoile
Like that star up above.'	Du bleu firmament!'
'Sir, I must obey you;	'J'obéis sans peine:
Off with my disguise!'	Tiens, regarde-moi.'
'O Heaven, it's the Queen!'	'Allah! C'est la Reine!'
Cried the King with surprise.	S'écria le roi!

EBOLI, THIBAULT AND LADIES-IN-WAITING

Ah! O pretty maidens, look to your veils, *etc.*	Ah! O jeunes filles, tissez des voiles! *etc.*

Elisabeth enters, coming out of the monastery. Scena and Ballade.

LADIES-IN-WAITING

The Queen!	La Reine!

EBOLI

(A mysterious sadness	(Une triste pensée
Clouds her days and fills her with sorrow.)	Tient toujours son âme oppressée.)

ELISABETH *seating herself beside the fountain*

I heard your song, gay and free from care . . .	Vous chantiez, libres de souci.
to herself	
(Alas! In days gone by, my heart was joyful too!)	(Hélas! Aux jours passés, j'étais joyeuse aussi!)

Rodrigo appears at the back. Thibault goes to him, speaks briefly to him in a low voice, and then returns to the Queen.

THIBAULT *introducing Rodrigo*

The Marquis of Posa begs to see you!	Le Marquis de Posa, Grand d'Espagne!

RODRIGO *bowing to the Queen*

My lady,	Madame,
I'm lately come from France and I bring you,	Pour Votre Majesté, par sa mère, à Paris,
From your mother, this letter entrusted to my care.	Ce pli fut en mes mains remis.

He gives the Queen a letter, and then adds in an undertone as he slips her a note with the letter:

This too! A letter from one who loves you!	Lisez: au nom du salut de votre âme!
indicating the letter to the ladies-in-waiting	
Behold the royal seal, with the crowned fleur-de-lys.	Voilà le sceau royal, la couronne et les lis!

Elisabeth remains motionless, confused, about to say something; a pleading look from Rodrigo disarms her.

EBOLI *to Rodrigo*

I'm so eager to hear the news you bring. The news from France, come, tell me everything!	[9] Que fait-on à la cour de France, Ce beau pays de l'élégance?

[9] ACT TWO Scena and Ballade

64

Se il tuo cor vorrai
A me dare in don,
Il mio trono avrai,
Ché sovrano io son.'
'Tu lo vuoi? t'inchina,
Appagar ti vo'.'
'Allah, La Regina!'
Mohammed sclamò.

Ah! Tessete i veli, vaghe donzelle,
etc.

La Regina!

       (Un'arcana mestizia
Sul suo core pesa ognora.)

Una canzon qui lieta risuonò.

(Ahimè! spariro i dì che lieto era il mio cor!)

*Nina Terentieva (Eboli) and Dale Wendel
(Thibault), Los Angeles Music Center
Opera, 1990 (photo: Frederic Ohringer)*

Il marchese di Posa, Grande di Spagna.

                       Signora,
Per Vostra Maestà, l'augusta madre un
    foglio
Mi confidò in Parigi.

Leggete, in nome della grazia eterna!

Ecco il regal suggel, i fiordalisi d'ôr.

Che mai si fa nel suol francese
Così gentil, così cortese?

65

RODRIGO *to Eboli*

All they talk of there is a ball,
Which they say will be attended by the King!

On s'occupe fort d'un tournoi,
Où, dit-on, paraîtra le Roi.

ELISABETH *the note in her hand*

(Ah! I do not dare. If I read it,
Will I be false to my vow?
Ah! I tremble!
In my soul I am blameless . . . God can see all my heart.)

(Ah! Je n'ose ouvrir! Il me semble
Que je forfais à l'honneur!
Quoi! Je tremble!
Mais mon âme est sans tâche, et Dieu lit dans mon coeur!)

EBOLI *to Rodrigo*

All the women of France, they tell us,
In grace and charm and kindness excel us.

Des Françaises rien ne surpasse,
Nous dit-on, l'esprit et la grâce.

RODRIGO *to Eboli*

It's far from true; here in Spain,
I find a princess more fair and twice as kind.

Vous seule avez, sous d'autres cieux,
Leur charme exquis et gracieux!

EBOLI *to Rodrigo*

At the Court, they say, when there's dancing,
Rows of beauties grandly appear,
Shining and fair, like goddesses entrancing.

Est-il vrai, qu'aux fêtes du Louvre,
Les déesses, choeur éclatant,
Semblent quitter le ciel qui s'ouvre?

RODRIGO *to Eboli*

None so bright as she before me here . . .

La plus belle y manque pourtant . . .

ELISABETH *reading*

'By the sacred memories which bind us,
By the name of all you hold dear,
By my life, in this man, as in me, you can trust. Carlos.'

'Par le souvenir qui nous lie,
Au nom de votre repos,
De ma vie, comme à moi, fiez-vous à cet homme — Carlos.'

EBOLI *to Rodrigo*

Is it true? At those dances, the ladies, or so I'm told,
Are dressed in silk or shining gold . . .

Pour le bal, on porte, je pense,
La soie et l'or de préférence . . .

RODRIGO *to Eboli*

Silk or gold, nothing can compare
With what our lovely princess chooses to wear!

Tout sied bien quand on est doté,
Princesse, de votre beauté!

ELISABETH *to Rodrigo*

Good! I thank you! You may ask a favour from the Queen.

Bien! Merci! Demandez une grâce à la Reine.

RODRIGO

I shall, but not for me!

J'accepte et non pour moi!

ELISABETH

(God, give me strength to bear it!)

(Je me soutiens à peine!)

EBOLI *to Rodrigo*

Who more worthy than you could seek reward or favour
From the Queen?

Qui plus digne que vous peut voir ses voeux comblés
Par la Reine?

D'un gran torneo si parla già,
E del torneo il Re sarà.

(Ah! non ardisco aprirlo ancor;
Se il fo, tradisco del Re l'onor.
Ah! Perché tremo?
Quest'alma è pura ancora. Dio mi legge
    in cor!)

Son le Francesi gentili tanto
E d'eleganza, di grazia han vanto.

In voi brillar sol si vedrà
La grazia insieme alla beltà.

È mai ver ch'alle feste regali,

Le Francesi hanno tali beltà,
Che solo in ciel trovan rivali?

La più bella mancar lor potrà . . .

'Per la memoria che ci lega,
In nome d'un passato a me caro,
V'affidate a costui, ven prego. Carlo.'

*Bernd Weikl (Rodrigo) and Claire Powell
(Eboli), Bayerische Staatsoper, Munich,
1989 (photo: Anne Kirchbach)*

Nei balli a Corte, pei nostri manti

La seta e l'ôr sono eleganti?

Tutto sta ben, allor che s'ha
La vostra grazia e la beltà.

Grata io son. Un favor chiedete alla
    Regina.

Accetto e non per me.

                    (Io mi sostengo appena!)

Chi più degno di voi può sue brame veder

Appagate?

ELISABETH

(I tremble!)   (Je tremble!)

EBOLI

Who can it be?   Expliquez-vous!

ELISABETH

Speak on!   Parlez!

RODRIGO

Carlos, my friend, hope of our future,	L'Infant Carlos, notre espérance,
Lives here in grief, and in despair.	Vit dans le deuil et dans les pleurs,
No one can guess his bitter suffering,	Et nul ne sait quelle souffrance
No hand relieves his burden of pain.	De son printemps flétrit les fleurs!
But you, his mother, you can console him,	O vous, sa mère, à ce coeur tendre
Bring him new comfort, give hope again.	Rendez la force et le repos . . .
Let him appear, say you'll receive him!	Daignez le voir, daignez l'entendre!
And save your son and calm his pain!	Sauvez l'Infant! Sauvez Carlos!

EBOLI

(One day as I stood by the side of my lady,	(Un jour, j'étais aux côtés de sa mère,
I saw the prince tremble and sigh beneath my glance.	J'ai vu l'Infant sous mes regards trembler,
Is he in love with me?)	Pâlir! . . . M'aimerait-il?)

ELISABETH

(How can I bear to see him! He is here! I'm afraid!)	(O destinée amère! Le revoir . . . je frémis!)

EBOLI

(Then why not tell his love?)   (Que n'ose-t-il parler?)

RODRIGO

Carlos the prince, spurned by his father,	L'Infant Carlos, du Roi son père,
Feels that his course on earth is run.	Trouva toujours le coeur fermé:
Spurned by the King! But who in the kingdom	Et cependant, qui sur la terre
More deserves his love than the King's own son?	Serait plus digne d'être aimé?
One word of love would cheer him,	Un mot d'amour à ce coeur tendre
Bring him new comfort, give hope again.	Rendrait la force et le repos.
Let him appear, say you will save him,	Daignez le voir, daignez l'entendre,
O save your son, o save the prince and calm his grief!	Sauvez l'Infant! Sauvez Carlos!

ELISABETH *to Thibault, with dignity and resolution*

Go! Say the Queen is here to receive her son!	Va! Je suis prête à recevoir mon fils!

EBOLI

(In love with me! Then why not dare to show his heart, and tell his love!)	(Ah! S'il m'aimait! . . . Et s'il osait m'ouvrir son coeur épris! . . .)

Rodrigo takes Eboli's hand, and they go off, talking softly. The ladies-in-waiting and pages leave.

Duet.

Don Carlos appears, slowly advances towards Elisabeth and bows to her without raising his eyes. Elisabeth, scarcely able to master her emotion, indicates that Don Carlos may approach. The Countess of Aremberg, who has remained behind, goes off, too, at a sign from Elisabeth.

DON CARLOS

I come before the Queen, and I ask for a favour,	Je viens solliciter de la Reine une grâce.
Knowing that she is loved by the King,	Celle qui dans le coeur du Roi

(Oh, terror!)

Ditelo, chi?

Chi mai?

Carlo, ch'è sol il nostro amore,
Vive nel duol su questo suol,
E nessun sa quanto dolore
Del suo bel cor fa vizzo il fior.
In voi la speme è di chi geme.
S'abbia la pace ed il vigor;
Dato gli sia che vi riveda;
Se tornerà, salvo sarà.

(Un dì che presso a sua madre mi stava

Vidi Carlo tremar . . .

Amor avria per me? . . .)

(La doglia in me s'aggrava,
Rivederlo è morir!)

(Perchè lo cela a me?)

Carlo del Re suo genitore
Rinchiuso il cor ognor trovò;
Eppur non so chi dell'amore

Saria più degno, ah! inver non so.

Un sol, un solo detto d'amore
Sparir il duolo farà dal cor;
Dato gli sia che vi riveda;
Se tornerà, salvo sarà.

Va! pronta io son il figlio a riveder.

(Oserà mai? potesse aprirmi il cor!)

Io vengo a domandar grazia alla mia Regina;

Quella che in cor del Re

Linda Finnie as Eboli, ENO, 1985 (photo: Catherine Ashmore)

That what she asks him will be granted.	Occupe la première place
She can alone obtain that favour I seek!	Seule peut obtenir cette grâce pour moi!
Here in Spain I'm dying, I am stifled, I am	[A]L'air d'Espagne me tue ... il me pèse, il
tortured.	m'opprime
Crushed in my soul by nameless horrors.	Comme le lourd penser d'un crime.
I must go, I must leave! Entreat the King	Obtenez ... il le faut, que je parte
	aujourd'hui
To send me to Flanders!	Pour la Flandre!

ELISABETH

My son!	Mon fils!

DON CARLOS

You call me son!	Pas ce nom-là! ... Celui
Another name was mine!	D'autrefois!

Elisabeth makes to go; Don Carlos beseeches her to stay.

Alas! Show pity!	Hélas, je m'égare!
Be kind! My wounded heart will break! O	Pitié! Je souffre tant! Pitié! Le ciel avare
cruel God,	
You revealed that dream of joy, and then	Ne m'a donné qu'un jour, et si vite il a
snatched it away!	fui!

ELISABETH

Prince, if the King is prepared	Prince, si le Roi veut se rendre
To grant what I shall ask him,	A ma prière ... pour la Flandre
He will send you to Flanders to rule in his	Par lui remise en votre main,
name.	Vous pourrez partir dès demain!
You will leave for Flanders today!	

Elisabeth makes a gesture of farewell to Don Carlos and makes to go.

DON CARLOS

Ah, not a word; you would send me	Quoi! Pas un mot, une plainte,
Into exile with no farewell!	Une larme pour l'exilé!
Calmly you turn aside and leave me,	Ah! Que du moins la pitié sainte
No glances of tender regret!	Dans votre regard m'ait parlé!
Alas! My soul is in torment ...	Hélas! Mon âme se déchire ...
Alas! In despair I'll die. Cruel heart!	Je me sens mourir ... Insensé!
So I have cried to a statue of marble,	J'ai supplié dans mon délire
Yes, marble, quite unfeeling and cold!	Un marbre insensible et glacé!

ELISABETH

Oh, Carlos, how can you call my heart	Carlos, n'accusez pas mon coeur
unfeeling and cruel?	d'indifférence.
Can you not tell why I'm stern, why I'm	Comprenez mieux sa fierté ... son
silent?	silence.
Like a flame, clear and bright, duty shines	Le devoir, saint flambeau, devant mes yeux
to light my path,	a lui,
And her light must be my guide.	Et je marche, guidée par lui,
For God alone can help and save me!	Mettant au ciel mon espérance!

DON CARLOS

O love, once mine, O love I lost!	[10] O bien perdu ... Trésor sans prix!
My one hope of joy, all I live for!	Ma part de bonheur dans la vie!

[10] CARLOS, *in a dying voice*

Ô bien per - du... Tré - sor sans prix! Ma part de bon-
Per - du - to ben, mio sol te - sor, ah! tu splen -
O love once mine, O love I lost! My one hope of

Tiene il posto primiero
Sola potrà ottener questa grazia per me!
Quest'aura m'è fatale, m'opprime, mi
   tortura,
Come il pensier d'una sventura.
Ch'io parta! n'è mestier! Andar mi faccia
   il Re
Nelle Fiandre.

      Mio figlio!

                Tal nome no . . . ma quel
D'altra volta!

              Infelice! più non reggo.
Pietà! Soffersi tanto; pietà! il ciel avaro

Un giorno sol mi die', poi rapillo a me!

Prence, se vuol Filippo udire
La mia preghiera, per la Fiandra da lui
Rimessa in vostra man
Ben voi potrete partir doman.

Ciel! non un sol, un sol detto,
Pel meschino ch'esul sen va!
Ah! perché mai parlar non sento
Nel vostro cor la pietà?
Ahimè! quest'alma è oppressa,
Ho in core un gel . . . Insan!
Piansi, pregai nel mio delirio,
Mi volsi a un gelido marmo d'avel!

Perché accusar il cor d'indifferenza?

Capir dovreste questo nobil silenzio.

Il dover, come un raggio al guardo mio
   brillò;
Guidata da quel raggio io moverò.
La speme pongo in Dio, nell'innocenza!

Perduto ben, mio sol tesor,
Ah! tu splendor di mia vita,

*Natalia Troitskaya (Elisabeth) and Plácido
Domingo (Don Carlos), Los Angeles Music
Center Opera, 1990 (photo: Frederic
Ohringer)*

-heur dans la vi - - - - - e!
-dor   di   mia vi - - - - - ta!
joy,   all   I   live _____   for!

Speak on, fill my soul with enchantment, For, when I hear your tender voice, paradise then is mine!	Parlez, parlez: enivrée et ravie, Mon âme, à votre voix, rêve du paradis!

ELISABETH

O God above, restore his heart! May he find repose and forget me! Carlos, farewell! We'll meet no more. Ah! Life beside you, paradise then were mine!	O Dieu clément, ce coeur sans prix, Qu'il soit consolé, qu'il oublie! Adieu, Carlos, dans cette vie, Ah! vivre auprès de vous c'était le paradis!

DON CARLOS

Heavenly wonder! My heart in its grief is consoled! And my pain and sorrow have vanished, And Heaven has been kind. At your feet in a dream of enchantment, I die!	O prodige! Mon coeur déchiré se console! Ma douleur poignante s'envole! Le ciel a pitié de mes pleurs ... [B]A vos pieds, éperdu de tendresse, je meurs!

He falls in a swoon on the grass.

ELISABETH *leaning over Don Carlos*

Mighty God! The life is dying In those eyes now filled with tears! Restore his heart, O God of Mercy! May his noble soul find repose! Alas! His sorrow overwhelms me, And in my arms, trembling and pale, Of love and of grief he is dying, The man to whom I was betrothed!	Dieu puissant, la vie est éteinte Dans son regard de pleurs voilé! Rendez le calme, ô bonté sainte! A ce noble coeur désolé! Hélas! Sa douleur me déchire, Entre mes bras, pâle et glacé, D'amour, de douleur, il expire, Celui qui fut mon fiancé!

DON CARLOS *in his delirium*

I hear a voice from Heaven! It calls [11] me back to life. I hear Elisabeth, my guardian angel, For you are by my side, as we were when first we met. And smiling spring has come to greet us with her flowers!	Par quelle douce voix, mon âme est ranimée? Elisabeth, c'est toi, ma bien-aimée, Assise à mes côtés, comme aux jours d'autrefois? Ah! Le printemps vermeil a reverdi les bois!

[11] CARLOS, *in a delirium*

Udir almen ti poss'ancor.
Quest'alma ai detti tuoi schiuder si vede
  il ciel!

Clemente Iddio, così bel cor,
Acqueti il suo duol nell'oblio,
O Carlo addio; su questa terra
Vivendo accanto a te mi crederei nel ciel!

O prodigio! Il mio cor s'affida, si consola;

Il sovvenir del dolor s'invola,
Il ciel pietà sentì di tanto duol.
Elisabetta, al tuo pie' morir io vo' d'amor.

Giusto ciel, la vita già manca
Nell'occhio suo che lagrimò.
Bontà celeste, deh! tu rinfranca
Quel nobil core che sì penò.
Ahimè! il dolor l'uccide,
Tra queste braccia io lo vedrò
Morir d'affanno, morir d'amore . . .
Colui che il ciel mi destinò!

Qual voce a me dal ciel scende a parlar
  d'amor?
Elisabetta! tu . . . bell'adorata,
Assisa accanto a me come ti vidi un dì!

Ah! il ciel s'illuminò, la selva rifiorì!

Maria Chiara (Elisabeth) and Luis Lima
(Don Carlos), Opernhaus-Zurich, 1979
(photo: Susan Schimert-Ramme)

ELISABETH

O what madness is this!
He is dying! O gracious Heaven!

O délire! O terreur!
Il expire! O bonté sainte!

DON CARLOS

From the peace of the tomb,
returning to his senses
I return to this life!
Why snatch me from death, cruel God!

A ma tombe fermée,

Au sommeil éternel
Pourquoi m'arracher, Dieu cruel!

ELISABETH

Carlos!

Carlos!

DON CARLOS

Under my feet let the earth crack asunder!
Out of the sky let the thunderbolt strike me!
I love you! Elisabeth, my love, the world is you alone!

Que sous mes pieds se déchire la terre!
Que sur mon front éclate le tonnerre,
Je t'aime, Elisabeth! Le monde est oublié!

He takes her in his arms.

ELISABETH *breaking free in alarm*

Will you strike and murder your father?
And then, still wet with his blood,
Will you lead to the altar your mother?

Eh bien! donc, frappez votre père!
Venez, de son meurtre souillé,
Traîner à l'autel votre mère!

DON CARLOS

Ah, cruel fate! I am cursed!

Ah! Fils maudit!

He flees, horror-struck.

ELISABETH

God above kept His watch over us!
falling to her knees
O God! O God!

Sur nous le Seigneur a veillé!

Seigneur! Seigneur!

Scena and Romance.

Thibault, Philip, the Countess of Aremberg, Rodrigo, the chorus, pages, enter in succession.

THIBAULT *coming in haste from the monastery*

The King!

Le Roi!

PHILIP ◊ *to Elisabeth*

Why alone here, my lady?
The Queen is not allowed to remain unattended!
Do you forget the rule of my Court?
Which of you ladies-in-waiting has failed in her task?

Pourquoi seule, Madame?
La Reine n'a pas même auprès d'elle une femme?
Ignorez-vous la règle de ma cour?
Quelle était aujourd'hui votre dame d'atour?

The Countess of Aremberg comes out from the crowd, trembling, and approaches the King.
to the Countess
Countess, you will go back to France tomorrow.

Comtesse, dès demain vous partez pour la France!

The Countess withdraws in tears. Everyone looks in surprise at the Queen.

CHORUS

Ah! What an insult to the Queen!

Ah! Pour la Reine quelle offense!

74

O delirio, o terror!
Egli muore! O ciel, ei muore!

Alla mia tomba,

Al sonno dell'avel
Sottrarmi perché vuoi, spietato ciel!

Carlo!

Sotto al mio pie' si dischiuda la terra,

Il capo mio sia dal fulmin colpito.

Io t'amo, Elisabetta! Il mondo è a me
sparito!

Compi l'opra, a svenar corri il padre,
Ed allor del suo sangue macchiato
All'altar puoi menare la madre.

Ah, maledetto io son!

Ah! Iddio su noi vegliò!

Signor! Signor!

*Richard Van Allan as Philip, ENO, 1985
(photo: Catherine Ashmore)*

Il Re!

Perché sola è la Regina?
Non una dama almeno presso di voi
serbaste?
Nota non v'è la legge mia regal?
Quale dama d'onor esser dovea con voi?

Contessa, al nuovo sol in Francia
tornerete.

Ah! La Regina egli offende!

◊ According to the *Disposizione Scenica*
Philip II is 'cold, sinister and stubborn
in character.'

ELISABETH *to the Countess of Aremberg*

Do not weep, my dear companion. [12] O ma chère compagne,
O dry those tears, though we so soon must Ne pleure pas, ma soeur.
   part.
Though from Spain you are banished, On te chasse d'Espagne,
You'll remain here within my heart. Mais non pas de mon coeur.
At your side I spent my childhood. Près de toi mon enfance
Those days will not come again! Passa ses jours joyeux!
To France you are returning. Tu vas revoir la France,
Ah! Greet that land from an exile in Ah! porte-lui mes adieux!
   Spain!
giving a ring to the Countess
Receive this ring and wear it, Reçois ce dernier gage
Recalling that in my heart you're dear. De toute ma faveur.
But conceal this wrong done me, Cache bien quel outrage
All the shame I'm forced to bear. Me couvre de rougeur.
Do not tell them of my suffering, Ne dis pas ma souffrance,
These tears of grief and pain. Les larmes de mes yeux.
To France you are returning. Tu vas revoir la France,
Ah! Greet that land from an exile in Ah! porte-lui mes adieux!
   Spain!

CHORUS, RODRIGO

Glistening tears attest Ah! C'est son innocence
That she is pure and blameless. Qui brille dans ses yeux.

PHILIP

(Boldly she dares defy me, (Avec quelle assurance
Pretends she's blameless.) Elle atteste les cieux!)

The Queen takes a tearful farewell of the Countess and leaves. The chorus follows her.

Duet. *

PHILIP *to Rodrigo, who is about to leave*

Remain! Restez!
Rodrigo stops, goes down on one knee to the King, then approaches him and dons his hat without any embarrassment.
I've seen you at my Court, sir, Auprès de ma personne
Yet you have never asked for an audience Pourquoi n'avoir jamais demandé d'être
   with me?   admis?
I am a man prepared to reward all my J'aime à récompenser ceux qui sont mes
   friends!   amis.
And my Posa, I'm told, served the Empire Vous avez, je le sais, bien servi ma
   most bravely!   couronne . . .

[12] ELISABETH, *to the Countess of Aremberg* - Romance

Non pianger, mia compagna,
Lenisci il tuo dolor.

Bandita sei di Spagna,
Ma non da questo cor.
Con te del viver mio
Fu lieta l'alba ancor;
Ritorna al suol natio,
Ti seguirà il mio cor!

Ricevi estremo pegno
Di tutto il mio favor;
Cela l'oltraggio indegno
Onde arrossisco ancor.
Non dir del pianto mio,
Del crudo mio dolor;
Ritorna al suol natio,
Ti seguirà il mio cor!

Spirto gentil e pio,
Acqueta il tuo dolor.

(Come al cospetto mio
Infinge un nobil cor!)

Louis Quilico as Rodrigo, Metropolitan Opera, 1983 (photo: Winnie Klotz)

Restate!

        Presso alla mia persona
Perché d'esser ammesso voi non
        chiedeste ancor?
Io so ricompensar tutti i miei difensor;

Voi serviste, lo so, fido alla mia corona . . .

* Verdi wrote four versions of the Philip/Rodrigo duet: it was partially rewritten before the Paris première in 1867, again for Naples in 1872, and once more for Milan in 1883/84. Each time the tone of the duet becomes more bitter, and closer to the comparable scene in Schiller's *Don Carlos*, which was the opera's principal source. (The final, Milan, version is given in the appendix).

RODRIGO

Why should I seek reward or favour from the King,
Sire? I live content beneath the law of your rule.

PHILIP

Pride is a thing I admire! Boldness a fault I can pardon,
If I wish! But I'm told you have left my army.
And men like Posa, who're born and bred as soldiers,
Are not contented living in peace!

RODRIGO

For my country my sword, tempered
By noble blood, has twenty times flashed from its scabbard.
Let Spain command, and I shall draw my sword again,
But let others bear the executioner's axe!

PHILIP

Marquis!

RODRIGO

Deign to hear me, Sire!
Since chance, since God
Decided to bring me before you this day,

The designs of providence
Would not have led me into your presence in vain.
One day you had to learn the truth!

PHILIP

Speak on!

RODRIGO

O King, I come here from Flanders,
From that country once so fair!
That is now but a desert of ashes,
A place of death and despair!
There in the streets there are orphans,
They're starving and beg for food,
Stumbling as they flee from the fire clouds,
Smeared with their own parents' blood!
The streams are laden with corpses,
The rivers with blood run red,
And the air is loud with shrieking
Of women who mourn for their dead.
Ah! Dear God be praised for this meeting!
Thy hand has led me to bring
The news of Flanders in torment
Before my King!

PHILIP

Blood is the price that's paid for peace in my dominions.
My thunderbolt has crushed those proud rebellious men,

Que pourrais-je envier de la faveur des rois,
Sire? Je vis content, protégé par nos lois.

J'aime fort la fierté . . . Je pardonne à l'audace . . .
Quelquefois . . . Vous avez délaissé mes drapeaux,
Et les gens comme vous, soldats de noble race,
N'ont jamais aimé le repos!

Pour mon pays, d'un noble sang trempée,
Mon épée a vingt fois brillé hors du fourreau.
Que l'Espagne commande et je reprends l'épée.
Mais d'autres porteront la hache du bourreau!

Marquis!

Daignez m'écouter, Sire!
Puisque le hasard, puisque Dieu
A voulu dans ce jour devant vous me conduire,
Les desseins de la providence, §
Ne m'auront pas en vain mis en votre présence!
Un jour vous aurez su la vérité!

Parlez!

O Roi! J'arrive de Flandre,
Ce pays jadis si beau!
Ce n'est plus qu'un désert de cendre,
Un lieu d'horreur, un tombeau!
Là, l'orphelin qui mendie
Et pleure par les chemins,
Tombe, en fuyant l'incendie
Sur des ossements humains!
Le sang rougit l'eau des fleuves,
Ils roulent, de morts chargés . . .
L'air est plein des cris des veuves
Sur les époux égorgés! . . .
Ah! La main de Dieu soit bénie,
Qui fait entendre par moi
Le glas de cette agonie
A la justice du Roi!

J'ai de ce prix sanglant payé la paix du monde;
Ma foudre a terrassé l'orgueil des novateurs,

78

Sperar che mai potrei dal favore del Re?

Sire, pago son io, la legge è scudo a me.

Amo uno spirto altier . . . L'audacia
   perdono . . .
Non sempre . . . Voi lasciaste il mestier
   della guerra;
Un uomo come voi, soldato d'alta stirpe,

Inerte può restar?

†

Pel patrio suol di nobil sangue intriso,
Più volte quest'acciar al sole scintillò.

Che la Spagna l'imponga, e snuderò
   la spada.
Ma ad altri del carnefice la scure lascerò.

Audace!

     Udir vogliate, o Sire!
Ora che il caso, or che Dio
Ha concesso in tal dì ch'io venissi a voi
   presso,
L'alto voler della provvidenza
Mi guidò non invan alla regal presenza!

Un dì nota vi fia la verità!

     Parlate!

O Signor, di Fiandra arrivo,
Da quel regno un dì si bel;
D'ogni ben or fatto privo
Sembra un carcer, un avel!
L'orfanel che non ha loco
Per le vie piangendo va;
Tutto struggon ferro e foco,
E bandita la pietà!
La riviera che rosseggia
Scorrer sangue al guardo par;
Della madre il grido echeggia
Pei figliuoli che spirar.
Ah! sia benedetto il cielo,
Che narrar lascia a me
Quest'agonia crudele,
Perché sia nota al Re.

Col sangue sol potei la pace aver del mondo;

Il brando mio calcò l'orgoglio ai novator,

† The changes in the words for Milan
commence at this point (see appendix).

§ Je ne joue, en parlant, que ma vie . . .
   et c'est peu.
Les desseins de la Providence,
A nos yeux trop souvent voilés,
Ne m'auront pas en vain mis en votre
   présence.

*Hans Hermann Nissen as Philip, Bayerische
Staatsoper, Munich, 1937 (photo:
Bildarchiv der Bayerische Staatsoper)*

Who sought to plunge our people in false, lying dreams!	Qui vont, plongeant le peuple en des rêves menteurs . . .
And death, sown by my own hands, has brought its harvest.	La mort, entre mes mains, peut devenir féconde.

RODRIGO

So! Do you believe that, sowing death, You sow for future peace?	Non! En vain votre foudre gronde! Quel bras a jamais arrêté La marche de l'humanité?

PHILIP

Look at Spain!	Le mien!

RODRIGO

A fiery wind has passed over the earth!	Un souffle ardent a passé sur la terre!
It has shaken all Europe!	Il a fait tressaillir l'Europe toute entière!
God proclaims to you His will:	Dieu vous dicte sa volonté,
Grant your subjects liberty!	Donnez à vos enfants la liberté!

PHILIP

Strange new way of speaking! Never, before my throne,	Quel langage nouveau! Jamais auprès du trône,
Has anyone thus raised his voice!	Personne n'éleva la voix si haut!
I have never before heard	Je n'avais jamais écouté
This unknown thing called truth!	Cette inconnue ayant pour nom, la vérité!
Rodrigo throws himself at the King's feet.	
raising Rodrigo	
No further word! Arise! You are young indeed,	Plus un mot! Levez-vous! Votre tête est bien blonde,
Since you invoke that deceitful phantom,	Pour que vous invoquiez le phantôme imposteur,
Before an old man, King of half the world!	Devant un vieillard, Roi de la moitié du monde!
Go, and beware my Inquisitor.	Allez et gardez-vous de mon Inquisiteur!

Rodrigo bows and makes to leave. After some hesitation, Philip recalls him hastily with a sign.

[No, remain, young man! I like your fiery ‡ spirit!	Non, reste, enfant! J'aime ton âme fière!
I will open all mine to yours! †	La mienne à toi va s'ouvrir tout entière! *
You have seen me on my throne, but not in my house!	Tu m'as vu sur mon trône, et non dans ma maison!
There all tells of treason.	Tout y parle de trahison.
The Queen, a suspicion torments me!	La Reine, un soupçon me torture!
My son!]	Mon fils!

RODRIGO

[His soul is noble and pure!]	Son âme est noble et pure!

PHILIP

[Nothing on earth is worth more than what he robbed from me!]	Rien ne vaut sous le ciel le bien qu'il m'a ravi!

RODRIGO

[What are you daring to say?]	Qu'osez-vous dire?

[13] PHILIP

Allegro moderato

Vo - tre re-gard har-di __ s'est le - vé __ sur mon trô - ne...
O - sò lo squar-do tu - o pe - ne-trar __ il mio so - glio.
You dared to lift your eyes and gaze on me __ as a ru - ler...

80

Ch'illudono le genti coi sogni mentitor.

Il ferro in questa man può divenir fecondo.

No! In van rugge la folgore!
Qual braccio fermar mai potrà
Nel suo cammin l'umanità?

Il mio!

Un soffio ardente avvivò questa terra,
E fè palpitar i popoli che serra!
Questa è di Dio la volontà,
O Re, date alle genti l'attesa libertà!

Quel favellar novel! Muto, sorpreso io sono,
Nessun si presso al trono udir fè questa voce!
Nessun svelato m'ha
La sconosciuta ai Re che ha nome verità!

Taci ormai, e sorgi! Si giovin tu sei,

Invocar tu non dei il fantasma impostor

Innanzi al vecchio Re, ch'ha la metà del mondo!
Va! Fuggi se puoi al grande Inquisitor!

No, resta qui! Amo il tuo spirto altero,

E il mio cuor a te s'aprirà!
Tu m'hai visto sul trono, e non in casa mia,

Ove ognuno è un traditore.
La Regina, un sospetto mi turba!
Mio figlio!

E un alma fiera e pura!

Nulla val sotto al ciel il ben ch'ei mi rapì!

Ch'osate dire?

‡ The passage in square brackets is a literal translation.

* The passage between * and * overleaf was cut before the Paris première in 1867.

† At this point in the Milan version (see p. 149) Verdi introduced the theme [13] discussed by Gilles de Van on p. 19.

allargando morendo

mais de ce front ou pè - se la cou-ron - ne sa - chez les tour-ments et le deuil!
Dal ca-po mio che gra-va la co - ro - na, l'an-go - scia ap-pren-di e il duol!
but did you see the hea-vy load of sor-row that weighs on the man b'neath the crown!

81

PHILIP

[My friend, be our judge,
Your counsel will be followed.
Be my guide, my refuge,
You, who alone are a man among mortals,

I wish to place my heart in your loyal
   hands!]

Ami, sois notre juge,
Ton conseil sera suivi.
Sois mon guide, mon refuge,
Toi, qui seul es un homme au milieu des
   humains,
Je veux mettre mon coeur en tes loyales
   mains!

RODRIGO

[This is a dream!]

C'est un rêve! *

PHILIP

[Young man! To my desolate heart
Return the peace long since banished.
In this blessed hour I find
The man long awaited!]

Enfant! A mon coeur éperdu,
Rends la paix dès longtemps bannie.
Je trouve à cette heure bénie
L'homme dès longtemps attendu!

RODRIGO

[(What Heaven-descended ray
Opens to me this pitiless heart?
I tremble at the perilous suspicion
Suspended over Carlos.)]

(Quel rayon du ciel descendu,
M'ouvre ce coeur impitoyable?
Je frémis du trait redoutable,
Sur Carlos déjà suspendu.)

PHILIP *to Lerma* §

[Henceforth the Marquis of Posa has access
To my presence at any time, in the
   palace!]

Le marquis de Posa peut entrer désormais,
Auprès de ma personne à toute heure, au
   palais!

RODRIGO

[(Almighty God, this is a dream!)]

(Dieu puissant, c'est un rêve! Ah!)

Philip leaves with Rodrigo, surrounded by courtiers who bow.

Nicolai Ghiaurov (Philip) and Mirella Freni (Elisabeth), Salzburg, 1979 (photo: Siegfried Lauterwasser)

Amico, sii nostro giudice,
Mi consiglia ti seguirò.
Sii mia guida, mio rifugio,
Tu, che sol sei un uom fra lo stuolo uman,

Vo' riporre il mio cuor nella leal tua man!

E'un sogno!

Mi rendi al cor dolente,
La pace che cercai.
Alfin, alfin trovai
Colui che l'alma ambì!

Qual lampo il ciel rischiara!
Quel cor s'apre all'affetto,
Io tremo del sospetto
Che Carlo mio colpì.)

Il signore di Posa, è mia volontà,
Presso di me a tutt'ora penetrare potrà.

(Sì, un sogno sembra a me! Ah!)

* End of the cut made prior to the Paris
première.

§ Verdi ignores the libretto's direction
'The Count of Lerma reenters with
several courtiers' and gives them no
music to sing. The libretto contains a
line addressed by Lerma to the
courtiers:
C'est un astre nouveau qui près du Roi
se lève!

*Nicolai Ghiaurov (Philip) and Piero Cappuccilli (Rodrigo), Salzburg, 1975 (photo: PSF/
Steinmetz)*

Act Three *

Introduction and Chorus.

Scene One. *The Queen's gardens in Valladolid. At the back, beneath an arcade, a statue with a fountain. Clear night. Ladies and gentlemen pass across the stage, on their way to the Queen's ball.* §

CHORUS *offstage*

Fragrant flowers, soft sparkling starlight,	Que de fleurs et que d'étoiles
Warm gentle breeze, sweet summer night!	Dans ces jardins tout embaumés!
While maidens fair, masking their beauty,	Que de beautés avec leurs voiles
Weave spells of love, tell of new delight!	Viennent s'offrir à nos yeux charmés!
Ah, soon the dawn will remind us,	Jusqu'au retour de l'aurore
Pleasure passes, all things are fleeting.	Tout est fête en ce beau séjour.
But may that dawn be slow to find us,	Puisse longtemps encore
Long may starlight shine on lovers meeting, ah!	Tarder du matin le retour,
	Ah! Tarder le retour
	Du jour!
Mandolines	Mandolines,
That tell of love,	Gais tambours,
Voices humming	Voix divines
An enchanted	Des amours,
Song of love,	Voix unies
Voices blending	Dans les airs,
With the breeze,	Harmonies,
Shadows stealing	Doux concerts,
Through the trees,	Voix touchante
Fingers strumming,	De la nuit,
Voices humming	Que tout chante!
An enchanted song of love.	Le temps fuit.

Elisabeth and Eboli enter on the last bars of the chorus. The Queen's women remain to one side.

ELISABETH

Come, Eboli. What though the night is scarcely beginning,	Viens, Eboli. La fête à peine est commencée,
Yet of these songs of joy already my sad soul wearies.	Et de son bruit joyeux déjà je suis lassée.
They expect far too much of me!	C'était trop exiger de moi!
The King, on the eve of his coronation,	Le Roi, que demain l'on couronne,
Passes the night in prayer to the Madonna.	Passe la nuit aux pieds de la madone.
Why should I not spend it in prayer?	Je vais prier comme le Roi!

EBOLI

But all the Court is here . . . The Prince . . .	Toute la Cour est là . . . l'Infant . . .

ELISABETH

Now take my cloak,	Prends ma mantille,
And my jewels, wear my black mask.	Mon collier, mon masque noir.
Charming Princess, when they see you,	En te voyant, chère fille,
All men will take you for me.	C'est moi que l'on croira voir.
Go, for my heart is yearning	Va! Je me sens dans l'âme
To be alone with my God.	La soif d'être avec Dieu.
And you can lead the dancing.	La fête te réclame.
Farewell!	Adieu!

* Act Two in the four-act Milan version. Because the Prelude, Introduction, Chorus and Ballet were not included, the second act of the Milan version begins, after a new prelude, at 'scene three' of the 1867 original.

§ De Lauzières, translating the libretto in 1867 into Italian, moved this and the following three scenes (the auto-da-fé, the King's study, the prison) to Madrid.

Quanti fior e quante stelle
Qui nei giardin e in fondo al ciel!

Quante a noi s'ascondon belle

Del mister sotto il vel!
Fin che nel ciel vien l'aurora
Tutto è gioia al regio ostello.
Possa tardar ancora
Il sol novello in ciel,
Ah! L'apparir
Del dì!

Mandoline,
Corde d'or,
Non vi tempri
Che l'amor.
Armonie
Dolci al cor,
Melodie
Liete ancor,
Fin che il giorno
Spunterà,
Sol v'ispiri
Voluttà.

Deh, vieni a me! La festa appena è
    cominciata,
E dal giulivo suon mi sento affaticata.

Era troppo pretender da me!
Il Re che doman dee cinger la corona
Presso l'altar, prega il Dio che perdona.

Supplice anch'io pregar vo' Dio!

Tutta la Corte è là . . . e Carlo . . .

                     Prend'il mio manto,
Il monil, la mia larva.
Tu resta qui; in te intanto
Me vedranno tratti in error.
Va, del mio cor la brama
E di pregar.
La festa ti reclama.
Addio!

*Rita Hunter as Elisabeth, ENO, 1975
(photo: John Garner)*

Elisabeth goes back into the palace. The Queen's women divide: two of them follow Elisabeth, and the others surround Eboli.

CHORUS †

Fragrant flowers, soft sparkling starlight, *etc.*	Que de fleurs et que d'étoiles, *etc.*

EBOLI

Now for one night I mean to reign here,	Pour une nuit me voilà Reine,
And wearing my mask till it's day,	Et dans ce jardin enchanté
I am the Queen and all obey me.	Je suis maîtresse et souveraine.
For am I not like that maiden,	Je suis comme la beauté
When we sang in the Veil Song,	De la légende du voile,
Wandering through the starry night,	Qui voit luire à son côté
To gain the man whom she loved best?	Le doux reflet d'une étoile!
Yes, I shall reign here till dawn!	Je vais régner jusqu'au jour!
Hidden by sweet veils of darkness,	Sous les doux voiles de l'ombre,
I plan to enchant my Carlos,	Je veux énivrer Carlos d'amour,
Fire his heart with love!	Le prince au coeur sombre!

Eboli gestures to a passing page, hands him a note that she writes hastily, and then leaves, followed by the Queen's women.

* Scene Two. The Ballet of the Queen: La Peregrina. *In a fairy grotto, all made of mother-of-pearl, coral and madrepore, wonderful pearls, the Indian Ocean's fairest, are assembled, hidden from all eyes. One of them, the Black Pearl, nonchalantly admires herself in a mirror held up to her by the Waves; another, the Pink Pearl, is trying on garlands of marine flowers in her tresses; the third, the White Pearl, is asleep in her shell.*

Suddenly a ray of dazzling light falls from on high into the realm of the Pearls; and in this ray there descends a glittering Spirit. The startled Pearls flee to their shells, which close on them. The Waves try in vain to sweep away the rash intruder who has dared to violate their mysterious kingdom. They feel their power shattered before that of the stranger. They flee.

The Spirit remains alone, disappointed, in the deserted grotto. All the Pearls have disappeared ... No ... The White Pearl is there, still asleep, stretched out in her shell. The Spirit sees her, admires her, and then, attracted by her beauty, approaches her and eventually plants a kiss on her brow. At this kiss, the Pearl wakes. She wishes to flee ... closes herself in her mother-of-pearl prison. The Spirit entreats her and wins her over ...

She consents to leave her shell; she complacently allows the Spirit to admire her, to take her in his arms ...

All the other Pearls, curious and envious, watch this spectacle from their half-open shells, and eventually bound out to defend their too carefree sister, with the result that the Spirit, dazzled by so many marvels, does not know to which he should give the prize.

However, the Waves have alerted the god Koral, the jealous guardian of the sea's treasures.

He arrives with an army. At the sight of him the Pearls tremble. The Spirit, despite the Pearls' entreaty, will be imprisoned for ever in the depths of the sea, beneath the guard of terrible monsters. In vain do the Pearls entreat. The god Koral is inexorable.

Spanish anthem: the Spirit is then transformed and becomes a Page with the arms and livery of Philip II.

The god Koral and the Pearls bow before one who represents the power of the ruler of half the world.

The Spirit tells the god Koral that he has come on his master's behalf to find the most beautiful pearl in the universe.

Finale: The god Koral brings forth for the Spirit all the marvels of his realm. The Spirit does not know which Pearl to choose, but the god, dissatisfied, wishes to fuse in one single Pearl the beauty of all.

At his command, all the treasures of the ocean's empire are cast in the shell of the White Pearl. The shell is transformed into a splendid chariot on which Elisabeth appears. This is the wonderful Pearl destined for the King of Spain, and everyone kneels before her to do her homage.

Quanti fior e quante stelle,
etc.

Per brev'ora io son Regina,
Ingannato dall'error
Ogni grande a me s'inchina.

Io son come la beltà
Della favola del vel,
Quando vide scintillar,
Il raggio d'una stella!

E fino all'alba ho da regnar!
Nel mistero io vo' d'amor,
Carlo il prence inebriar,
Il prence inebriar d'amor!

† The reprise of the offstage chorus was cut before the Paris première in 1867.

* The ballet contains about fifteen minutes of music and is often cut in performance. The Paris libretto contains a different scenario, which ends with the appearance of 'La Pérégrina', 'the most beautiful jewel in the Crown of Spain. This pearl, unrivalled except by that of Cleopatra, is personified by the Queen. Eboli, wearing her mask and her mantilla, appears in a glittering chariot, the Spanish anthem sounds, the Pearls kneel, the Lords and Ladies at the ball bow to pay homage to their sovereign.'

Grace Bumbry as Eboli, Houston Grand Opera, 1982 (photo: Jim Caldwell)

Scene Three. *

Duet and Trio.

DON CARLOS *reading a note*

'At midnight, in the garden of the Queen, You'll find me there, beyond the fountain . . .'	'A minuit, aux jardins de la Reine, § Sous les lauriers, auprès de la fontaine . . .'
It is midnight! I hear In the darkness the sound of the murmuring waters.	Il est minuit! J'entends Le bruit clair de la source au milieu du silence.
Drunk with my love, filled with delight and longing,	Ivre d'amour, plein d'une joie immense,
Elisabeth, my love, ah, my life, I am here!	Elisabeth! mon bien, mon bonheur . . . Je t'attends!

Ebol appears, veiled.
to Eboli: he takes her for Elisabeth

You're mine! My own beloved! Walking here amid these flowers. You're mine, my soul is enchanted, All of the future, all is ours. O radiant star who'll ever guide me, In days of grief my sacred shrine. That grief has flown now you're beside me. My love, ah, my life, you're mine!	C'est vous! Ma bien-aimée Qui marchez parmi ces fleurs. C'est vous! Mon âme charmée Voit s'envoler ses douleurs. O source ardente et sacrée De mon bonheur le plus doux, De ma tristesse adorée, Mon bien, mon amour, c'est vous!

EBOLI

(A love like his is the dream I've longed for.	(Un tel amour, c'est le bien suprême!
Ah! How sweet to be loved by him!)	Il est doux d'être aimée ainsi!) §§

DON CARLOS

In a dream let us live, forgetting all the future!	Oublions l'univers, la vie et le ciel même!
Farewell, cares of the world! One thing alone remains:	Qu'importe le passé? Qu'importe l'avenir?
I love you!	Je t'aime!

EBOLI

Ever united, we shall live for our love!	Puisse l'amour à jamais nous unir!

She takes off her mask.

DON CARLOS *horrified*

(Ah! What have I said?)	(Dieu! Ce n'est pas la Reine!)

EBOLI

O Heaven! What sudden terror makes you tremble? You avoid me, and you fall into silence!	O ciel! Quelle pensée Vous tient pâle, immobile et la lèvre glacée?
What spectre has troubled your soul? Can you doubt that my heart beats with passion for you?	Quel spectre se lève entre nous? Doutez-vous de ce coeur, qui ne bat que pour vous?

'A mezzanotte, ai giardin della Regina,
Sotto gli allor della fonte vicina.'

§ On me dit 'A minuit, aux jardins de
la Reine,'

E mezzanotte;
Mi par udir il mormorio del vicino fonte.

Ebbro d'amor, ebbro di gioia il core!

Elisabetta! mio ben! mio tesor! a me vien!

Sei tu, bell'adorata
Che appari in mezzo ai fior!
Sei tu! l'alma beata
Già scorda il suo dolor!
O tu cagion del mio contento,
Parlarti posso almen!
O tu cagion del mio tormento
Sei tu, amor mio, sei tu, mio ben!

(Un tanto amor è gioia a me suprema!

Amata, amata io son!)

§§ This line is not in the libretto.

L'universo obliam! te sola, o cara, io
bramo!
Passato più non ho, non penso all'avvenir!

Io t'amo!

Possa l'amor il tuo cor al mio cor sempre
unir!

(Ciel! Non è la Regina!)

Ahimè! Qual mai pensiero

*Diagram from the 'Disposizione Scenica':
Don Carlos enters at B, holding a letter:
while he is reading, Eboli enters from C
and remains in the background. At the
words 'I am here', Carlos turns and catching
sight of Eboli, whom he takes to be the
Queen, goes to her and says with fire and
tenderness: 'You're mine! My own beloved!'*

Vi tien pallido, immoto, e fa gelido il
labbro?
Quale spettro si leva tra noi?
Non credete al mio cor, che sol batte per
voi?

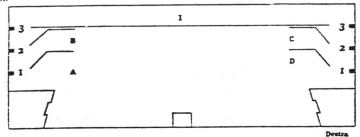

89

Alas! Your youthful mind has no idea
What dangers lurk along the path you
  tread.
You have not heard that distant thunder,
Nor seen the lightning gather round your
  head!

Hélas! Votre jeunesse ignore
Quel piège affreux on dresse sur vos pas;
§
J'entends la foudre qui dévore
Sur votre front déjà gronder tout bas!

DON CARLOS

Well I know that hidden dangers
Lurk along the lonely path I tread.
My ears have heard that distant thunder,
And the lightning gathers round my head!

Ne croyez pas que j'ignore
Les périls semés sous mes pas.
J'entends la foudre qui dévore
Sur ma tête gronder tout bas!

EBOLI

I must warn you that your trusted Posa
Is always with your father, talking of you!
But I can save you, since I love you!

Votre père . . . et Posa lui-même
Souvent tout bas de vous ont parlé!
Je puis vous sauver . . . Je vous aime!

DON CARLOS

Rodrigo! This mysterious warning fills
  my soul with fear!

Rodrigue! Quel mystère ici m'est dévoilé?

EBOLI *anxious*

O Carlos!

Carlos!

DON CARLOS

Ah! Though your heart is good and noble,
Know that mine is forever cold, closed to
  thoughts of joy.
We were both led astray by dreams of
  madness,
Wrought by the spell of night, and the scent
  of the flowers!

Ah! Vous avez le coeur d'un ange,
Mais le mien pour jamais dort, au bonheur
  fermé. §§
Nous avons fait tous deux un rêve étrange,

Par cette belle nuit, sous les bois embaumés!

EBOLI

Of madness? O God! Then those words
  that you uttered,
Words of burning passion, were meant for
  another?
I can guess who she is! The Queen!

Un rêve! O ciel! Ces paroles de flamme,

Vous croyez les dire à quelque autre
  femme?
Quel éclair! Quel secret!

DON CARLOS *horrified*

                  Forbear!

                        Pitié!

Rodrigo enters.

RODRIGO

You are mad if you can believe that!
Can you not see? He's out of his mind!

Que dit-il? Il est en délire . . .
Ne croyez pas cet insensé!

EBOLI

I looked in his heart, saw its depths!
Carlos is doomed, cannot be saved!

Au fond de son coeur j'ai su lire!
Et son arrêt est prononcé!

RODRIGO

What do you mean?

Qu'a-t-il dit?

EBOLI

                Let me go!

                Laissez-moi!

RODRIGO

    What do you mean? Wretched woman,
Tremble, for I . . .

           Qu'a-t-il dit? Malheureuse,
Tremble! Je suis . . .

V'è ignoto forse, ignoto ancora
Qual fier agguato a' piedi vostri sta?

§ Le périls semés sous vos pas;

Sul vostro capo ad ora, ad ora
La folgore del ciel piombar potrà!

Deh! nol credete: ad ora, ad ora
Più denso vedo delle nubi il vel;
Su questo capo io veggo ognora
Pronta a scoppiar la folgore del ciel!

Udii dal padre, da Posa istesso
In tuon sinistro di voi parlar.
Salvarvi poss'io. Io v'amo!

Rodrigo! Qual mistero a me si rivelò!

Ah! Carlo!

§§ Mais le mien pour jamais dort, à
l'amour fermé.

            Il vostro inver celeste è un core,
Ma chiuso il mio restar al gaudio de'!

Noi facemmo ambedue un sogno strano,

In notte sì gentil tra il profumo dei fior.

Un sogno! O ciel! Quelle parole ardenti

Ad altra credeste rivolgere illuso!

Qual balen! Qual mister!

                        Pietà!

Che disse mai?! Egli delira,
Non merta fè! Demente egli è!

Io nel suo cor lessi l'amor;
Or noto è a me. Ei si perdé!

Che vuoi dir?

            Tutto io so!

                Che vuoi dir? Sciagurata!
Trema! io son …

*Torsten Ralf (Don Carlos) and Gertrud
Rünger (Eboli), Bayerische Staatsoper,
Munich, 1937; conductor, Clemens Krauss,
producer, Rudolf Hartmann, designer,
Rochus Gliese (photo: Bildarchiv der
Bayerische Staatsoper)*

EBOLI

You are the King's new friend.
Yes, I know that, but in me you have a foe,
And I am dangerous!

I know all of your power ... you cannot
    guess at mine!

RODRIGO

What are you trying to tell me?

EBOLI

Nothing!
He's in my power, you cannot save him!
Now he has scorned the love I gave him!

RODRIGO *to Eboli*

Confess, and let us learn your power!
What were you doing here at this hour?

EBOLI

I turn at bay like a tigress wounded!
Beware of a woman offended!

RODRIGO

Beware the wrath of God above!
He will protect innocent love!

DON CARLOS

O my grief! I have lost my honour!
I've besmirched the name of my mother!
God in mercy looks down from above!
He will shield our innocent love!

EBOLI

And I used to tremble before her!
Though she was robed in a mantle of virtue,
Though she walked through the Court with
    the air of a saint,
All the while she was greedily draining
The cup of the pleasures of passion!
Ah! By my faith, now the King shall hear
    this!

RODRIGO *drawing his dagger*

If you should dare!

DON CARLOS *stopping him*

Rodrigo!

RODRIGO

Those accursed
Lips of hers must swallow their poison for
    ever!

DON CARLOS

Rodrigo, the King!

EBOLI

Do you fear to strike me?
Why do you shrink from the blow? Here I
    am!

Le favori du Roi!
Oui, je le sais, mais je suis, moi,
Une ennemie dangereuse! §

Je sais votre pouvoir ... Vous ignorez le
    mien.

Que prétendez-vous dire?

Rien!
Redoutez tout de ma furie!
Entre mes mains je tiens sa vie!

Parlez et dévoilez ainsi
Ce qui vous a conduite ici!

Ah! La lionne au coeur est blessée!
Craignez une femme offensée!

Craignez d'armer le Dieu puissant,
Ce protecteur de l'innocent!

Qu'ai-je-fait? O douleur amère!
J'ai flétri le nom de ma mère!
Le regard du Dieu tout-puissant
Seul reconnaîtra l'innocent!

Et moi qui tremblais devant elle!
Elle voulait, cette sainte nouvelle,
Des célestes vertus, conservant les dehors,

S'abreuver à pleins bords
A la coupe où l'on boit les plaisirs de la vie!
Ah! sur mon âme, elle était hardie!

Malheur à toi!

Rodrigue!

Le poison
N'est pas encor sorti de sa lèvre maudite!

Rodrigue, calme-toi!

Votre main hésite?
Que tardez-vous à frapper? ... me voilà!

92

L'intimo sei del Re,
Ignoto non è a me.
Ma una nemica io son formidabil,
   possente:
M'è noto il tuo poter, il mio t'è ignoto
   ancor!

§ Une ennemie aussi vaillante et
dangereuse!

Che mai pretendi dir?

Nulla!
Al mio furor sfuggite invano.
Il suo destin è in questa mano.

Parlar dovete, a noi svelate
Qual mai pensiero vi trasse qui.

Io son la tigre al cor ferita,
Alla vendetta l'offessa invita.

Su voi del ciel cadrà il furor.
Degli innocenti è il protettor.

Stolto fui! Oh, destin spietato!
D'una madre ho il nome macchiato!
Sol Iddio indagar potrà,
Se questo cor colpa non ha.

Ed io, che tremava al suo aspetto!
Ella volea, questa santa novella,
Di celesti virtù mascherando il suo cor,

Il piacere libar ed intera
La coppa vuotar dell'amor.
Ah per mia fé! fu ben ardita!

Tu qui morrai.

Rodrigo!

Il velen
Ancora non stillò quel labbro maledetto!

Shirley Verrett as Eboli, Covent Garden,
1967 (photo: Reg Wilson)

Rodrigo! frena il cor!

Perché tardi a ferir?
Non indugiar ancor! . . . Perché tardi?

RODRIGO *throwing down his dagger*

No! Sudden hope inspires me, and God
   will be my guide!

Non! Un espoir me reste et Dieu me
   conduira!

EBOLI *to Don Carlos*

Treacherous son, adulterous lover,
For my revenge I mean to cry . . .
What you have done admits no pardon.
When I reveal it you must die!

[14] Malheur sur toi, fils adultère,
Mon cri vengeur va retentir . . .
Malheur sur toi, demain la terre
S'entr'ouvrira pour t'engloutir.

RODRIGO *to Eboli*

If you should speak, then God will strike
   you,
Raising His arm to prove you lie!
If you should speak, He'll show no mercy.
He will strike and you will die!

Si vous parlez, qu'un Dieu sévère

Lève son bras pour vous punir!
Si vous parlez, ah! puisse la terre
S'entr'ouvrir pour vous engloutir!

DON CARLOS

Everything's lost! She knows my secret!
O God in mercy, hear my cry!
Everything's lost! She knows my secret!
Merciful God, oh let me die!

Elle sait tout! O peine amère!
Douleur dont je me sens mourir!
Elle sait tout! Ah! Que la terre
S'entr'ouvre enfin pour m'engloutir!

Eboli leaves in a fury.

RODRIGO

My Carlos, if you are carrying any
   dangerous papers . . .
Any letters . . . or plans . . . to me you must
   entrust them!

Carlos, si vous avez quelque importante
   lettre . . .
Quelques notes . . . des plans . . . il faut me
   les remettre!

DON CARLOS *hesitating*

To you? . . . The favourite of the King?

A vous? . . . au favori du Roi?

RODRIGO

Is Carlos mistrustful of me?

Carlos, tu doutes de moi?

DON CARLOS

No! O my friend, my dear companion!
My love for you cannot fail.
You know this heart is yours forever.
My friend, whom I trust as a brother,
Here! All the plans I have made, here they
   are!

Non! Mon appui . . . mon espérance!
Ce coeur qui t'a tant aimé
Ne te sera jamais fermé.
En toi j'ai toujours confiance . . .
Tiens . . . mes papiers importants, les
   voici!

RODRIGO

Carlos, my friend!
Ah! You may trust in my love!

O mon Carlos!
O mon cher prince, merci!

DON CARLOS

I place my life in your hands!

Ah! Je me livre à toi!

They throw themselves into one another's arms.

[14] EBOLI

No, una speme mi resta: m'ispirerà il
  Signor.

Trema per te, falso figliuolo,
La mia vendetta arriva già.
Trema per te, fra poco il suolo
Sotto il tuo pie' si schiuderà!

Tacer tu dêi; rispetta il duolo,

O un Dio severo ti punirà.
Tacer tu dêi; o per te il suolo
Sotto il tuo pie' si schiuderà.

Tutto ella sa! tremendo duolo!
Oppresso il cor forza non ha.
Tutto ella sa! Né ancora il suolo
Sotto il mio piè si schiuderà?

Carlo, se mai su te fogli importanti serbi,

Qualche nota, un segreto, a me affidarli dêi.

A te! All'intimo del Re?

Sospetti tu di me?

No, no, del mio cor sei la speranza;
Questo cor che sì t'amò
A te chiudere non so.
In te riposi ogni fidanza;
Sì, questi fogli importanti ti do!

Carlo, tu puoi,
Tu puoi fidare in me.

Io m'abbandono a te.

*Blanche Thebom as Eboli (photo: Royal
Opera House Archives)*

-geur   va   re - ten - tir...
-det - ta a r - ri - va   già.
-venge I   mean   to   cry.

Scene four.* *A large square before Valladolid Cathedral. Right, the church, approached by a large flight of steps; left, a palace; at the back, another flight of steps leads to a lower square, large buildings and distant hills form the background.*

Finale. [15]

Bells ring out. The crowd surges onto the square.

THE PEOPLE

Today is a day of gladness and joy,
Today is the day we greet and praise our
   king of kings!
The world unites to sing his praises,
Every land must own him as master!
Our great love will be with him always.
Was ever love more richly earned?
His name is the pride of Spain,
And that name will live for ever in glory!

Ce jour heureux est plein d'allégresse!
Honneur au plus puissant des Rois!

Le voeu du monde à lui s'adresse.
Le monde est courbé sous ses lois!
Notre amour partout l'accompagne,
Jamais amour plus mérité;
Son nom est l'orgueil de l'Espagne,
Il vivra dans l'éternité!

A funeral march is heard. Monks cross the square, leading the men condemned by the Inquisition.

THE MONKS

Today is a day of repentance,
A day of wrath, a day of fear,
Of grief to guilty wretches,
Who have dared to offend the sacred laws
   of God!
Yet Holy Church will grant her pardon,
If once the sinner confess his crime,
And repent when death is approaching,
When the flames have consumed his pride!

Ce jour est un jour de colère,
Un jour de deuil, un jour d'effroi.
Malheur au téméraire
Qui du ciel a bravé la loi!

Mais le pardon suit l'anathème
Si le pécheur épouvanté
Se repent à l'heure suprême
Sur le seuil de l'éternité!

They go off.

THE PEOPLE

Glory, praise to our king of kings!
etc.
Long live the King!

Honneur au plus puissant des Rois!
etc.
Honneur au Roi!

March.

[15] ACT THREE - Finale

96

Spuntato ecco il dì d'esultanza;
Onore al più grande dei Regi!

In esso hanno i popol fidanza,
Il mondo è prostrato al suo piè!
Il nostro amor ovunque l'accompagna,
E questo amor giammai non scemerà.
Il nome suo è l'orgoglio della Spagna,
E viver deve nell'eternità!

Il dì spuntò, dì del terrore,
Il dì tremendo, il dì feral.
Morran! giusto gli è il rigor
Dell'immortal.

Ma di perdon voce suprema
All'anatema succederà
Se il peccator all'ora estrema
Si pentirà!

Spuntato è il dì d'esultanza!
etc.
Onor al Re!

* Scene two in the Milan version. The Italian versions give the setting for this scene as Our Lady of Atocha in Madrid, the scene of royal ceremonies in the capital. Valladolid cathedral had not been built at the time of the opera, but Valladolid was Philip's centre of government in 1560 and there was a well-documented auto-da-fé in the Plaza Mayor on May 21, 1559. Descriptions of this certainly influenced the conception and design of this scene in the Paris première.

Diagram from the 'Disposizione Scenica'. On the right, the church G approached by a broad flight of steps, E and F. R are steps leading to another square where a pyre H has been erected of which the top is visible. On the left is a palace with a large porch, J. K is a balcony for the military band. At the back is a cloth showing great buildings and distant hills. The stage has very great depth of background, and is flooded with light. As the curtain rises, the crowd rushes on, and is held back with difficulty by the guards.

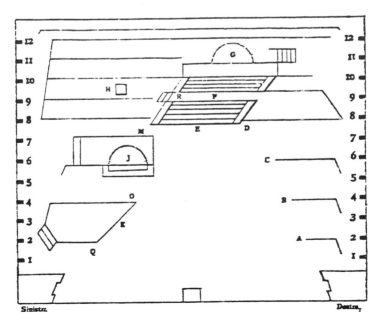

The procession comes out of the palace; all the officers of state, all the Court, deputies from every province of the Empire, the Grandees of Spain, Rodrigo among them; the Queen, surrounded by her ladies; Thibault, bearing Elisabeth's train, pages, etc.

THE ROYAL HERALD *before the doors of the church, which remain closed.*

Let the sacred doors now be opened,	Ouvrez-vous, ô portes sacrées!
The house of the Lord be revealed!	Maison du Seigneur, ouvre-toi!
O silent great cathedral,	O voûtes vénérées,
Now restore us our King.	Rendez-nous notre Roi!

THE PEOPLE

Let the sacred doors now be opened,	Ouvrez-vous, ô portes sacrées!
etc.	*etc.*

The doors of the church as they open reveal Philip, crowned, advancing beneath a canopy, with monks around him. The lords bow and the people kneel.

PHILIP *beneath the canopy*

When I placed on my head this sacred crown,	En plaçant sur mon front, Peuple, cette couronne,
I gave my solemn word to God whose hand bestowed it,	J'ai fait serment au Dieu qui me la donne
That all His foes I'd destroy by fire and sword!	De la venger par le fer et par le feu!

THE PEOPLE

Long live the King! Praise to God!	Gloire à Philippe! Gloire à Dieu!

Everyone bows for a moment in silence. Philip descends the steps of the church and takes Elisabeth's hand to continue his progress. Suddenly the Flemish deputies appear, led by Don Carlos, and throw themselves at Philip's feet.

ELISABETH

(O Heaven! It's Carlos!)	(O ciel! Carlos!)

RODRIGO

(This will lead to disaster!)	(Qu'ose-t-il entreprendre?)

PHILIP

Who are these men before me on their knees?	Qui sont ces gens courbés à mes genoux?

DON CARLOS

They have been sent from Brabant and from Flanders,	Des députés du Brabant, de la Flandre,
And I, your son, have led them to the King!	Que votre fils amène devant vous!

SIX FLEMISH DEPUTIES

Hear us, hear us, Sire!	Sire, la dernière heure
Must Flanders cry in vain?	A-t-elle donc sonné pour vos sujets flamands?
All your subjects implore you in their grief and distress.	Tout un peuple qui pleure
Oh, help us in our pain!	Vous adresse ses cris et ses gémissements!
When you knelt in the house of God,	Si votre âme attendrie
Did His voice not inspire your heart to peace in your land?	A puisé la clémence et la paix au saint lieu,
Then spare our noble country,	Sauvez notre patrie,
Mighty King, which God Himself did entrust to your hand!	O Roi puissant, vous qui tenez la puissance de Dieu!

Schiusa or sia la porta del tempio!
O magion del Signor, t'apri omai!
Sacrario venerato,
A noi rendi il nostro Re!

During the chorus, the King descends the stairs E and comes into the centre of the stage.

Schiusa or sia la porta del tempio!
etc.

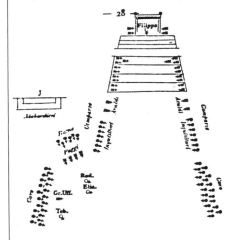

Nel posar sul mio capo la corona,

Popol, giurai al ciel, che me la dona,

Dar morte ai rei col fuoco e con l'acciar.

Gloria a Filippo! Gloria al ciel!

(Qui Carlo! O ciel!)

(Qual pensier lo sospinge!)

Chi son costor prostrati innanzi a me?

Son messagger del Brabante e di Fiandra

Che il tuo figliuol adduce innanzi al Re.

Sire, no, l'ora estrema
Ancora non suonò per i Fiamminghi in
    duol.
Tutto un popol t'implora,

Fa che in pianto così sempre non gema.
Se pietoso il tuo core
La clemenza e la pace chiedea nel
    tempio,
Pietà di noi ti prenda, e salva il nostro suol,
O Re, che avesti il tuo poter da Dio.

PHILIP

To God, the Flemings are unfaithful,
And their King they disobey.
And they rebel, rise up against me.
Soldiers, seize them! And take these traitors
away!

A Dieu vous êtes infidèles
Infidèles à votre Roi.
Ces suppliants sont des rebelles.
Gardes! Eloignez-les de moi!

SIX MONKS

Men of Flanders are always faithless,
The laws of God they disobey.
They break God's laws, the men of Flanders,
And they rebel against the King!

Les Flamands sont des infidèles,
Ils ont bravé, bravé la loi;
Ces suppliants sont des rebelles;
Que votre coeur les juge, ô Roi!

ELISABETH, DON CARLOS, RODRIGO, THIBAULT, THE PEOPLE

May the King in his grace grant them mercy
and pardon.
Pity the men who live in that suffering
place,
Who groan and weep beneath your heavy
chain,
Whom to death you condemn. Oh, grant
them grace!

Etendez sur leurs fronts votre main
souveraine,
Sire, prenez pitié d'un peuple infortuné,

Qui va, sanglant, traînant sa chaîne,

Au désespoir, à la mort condamné!

The King wishes to proceed. Don Carlos bars his way.

DON CARLOS

Sire, I have something to ask you!
Must I spend all my youth leading a
useless existence
Here at your Court?
And since God will bestow one day on
my brow
That noble imperial crown,
For that duty prepare me, ensure that I am
worthy!
Let me rule
In Brabant and in Flanders!

Sire, il est temps que je vive!
Je suis las de traîner une jeunesse oisive

Dans votre cour.
Si Dieu veut qu'à mon front un jour

La couronne d'or étincelle,
Préparez à l'Espagne un maître digne
d'elle!
Confiez-moi
Le Brabant et la Flandre!

PHILIP

Are you mad that you dare suggest it?
You ask that I should give you a sword,
A sword that you can raise against the King
himself!

Insensé! qu'oses-tu prétendre?
Tu veux que je te donne, à toi,
Le fer qui, tôt ou tard, immolerait le Roi!

DON CARLOS

Ah! God reads all our hearts. God alone
can judge our actions!

Ah! Dieu lit dans nos coeurs, Dieu nous a
jugés, Sire!

ELISABETH

(I tremble!)

(Je tremble!)

RODRIGO

(The prince is lost!)

(Il est perdu!)

DON CARLOS *drawing his sword*

Then by God, with my sword,
Here I stand for the people of Flanders
myself!

Par le Dieu qui m'entend,
Je serai ton sauveur, noble peuple flamand!

ELISABETH, THIBAULT, RODRIGO, THE MONKS, THE PEOPLE

A sword before the King! The prince has
lost his senses!

Le fer devant le Roi! L'Infant est en délire!

100

A Dio voi foste infidi,
Infidi al vostro Re,
Son i Fiamminghi a me ribelli:
Guardie, vadan lontan da me.

Ah, son costor infidi,
In Dio non han la fè,
Vedete in lor sol dei ribelli!
Tutto il rigor mertan del Re!

Su di lor stenda il Re la sua mano sovrana,

Trovi pietà, signor, il Fiammingo nel
    duol:
Nel suo martir presso a morir,

Ei manda già l'estremo suo sospir.

Sire! egli è tempo ch'io viva!
Stanco son di seguir un'esistenza oscura

In questo suol!
Se Dio vuol che il tuo serto

Questa mia fronte
Un giorno a cinger venga,

Per la Spagna prepara un Re degno di lei!
Il Brabante e la Fiandra a me tu dona.

Insensato! Chieder tanto ardisci!
Tu vuoi ch'io stesso porga
A te l'acciar che un dì immolerebbe il Re!

Ah! Dio legge a noi nel cor; Ei giudicarci de'.

(Io tremo!)

        (Ei si perdé!)

                Io qui lo giuro al ciel!
Sarò tuo salvator, popol fiammingo, io sol!

L'acciar! Innanzi al Re! L'Infante è fuor di
    sé.

Carlos rushes in from B, followed by six Flemish Deputies who group themselves in two rows and throw themselves at Philip's feet.

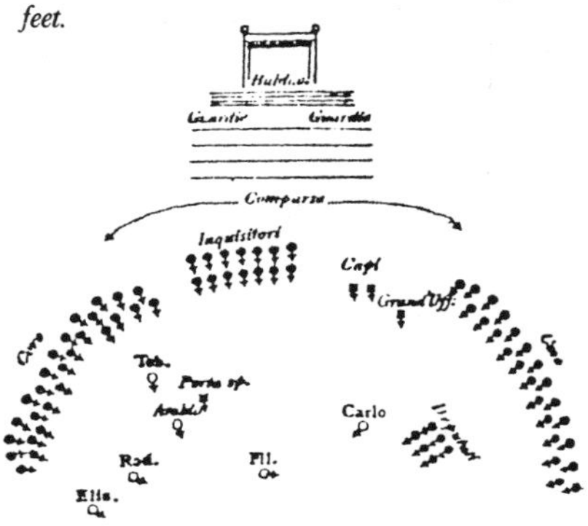

101

PHILIP

Guards! Now disarm the prince!
My lords, defenders of my throne,
Let the prince be disarmed! What! You
  dare not!

Gardes! Désarmez l'Infant!
Seigneurs, soutiens de mon trône,
Désarmez l'Infant! . . . Quoi! Personne!

DON CARLOS

Ah, who will dare to take my life?
I am prepared to sell it dearly!

J'attends celui qui l'osera,
A me venger ma main est prête!

The Grandees of Spain retreat before Don Carlos.

PHILIP

Must I do so myself!

Désarmez l'Infant!

RODRIGO *to Don Carlos*

Yield your sword, sir!

Votre épée!

ELISABETH

       O Heaven!

       O ciel!

DON CARLOS

      You, Rodrigo!

      Toi, Rodrigue!

Don Carlos hands his sword to Rodrigo, who bows as he presents it to the King.

THE PEOPLE

      He! Posa!

      Lui! Posa!

ELISABETH

He!

Lui!

PHILIP

Marquis, I make you Duke! Light the
  flames to Heaven's glory!

Marquis, vous êtes Duc! . . . Maintenant, à
  la fête!

The King leaves, giving his hand to the Queen. All the Court follows him. They go to take up their places on the grandstand that has been reserved for them for the auto-da-fé.

Reprise of the choruses of the People and the Monks.

A HEAVENLY VOICE

O fly to Heaven above, o fly, poor souls
 . that burn in torment!
Draw nigh to the throne of love,

Where peace will always invite you!

Volez vers le Seigneur, volez, ô pauvres
  âmes!
Venez goûter la paix près du trône de
  Dieu!
Le pardon!

THE FLEMISH DEPUTIES

Can God allow this shame! Will He not
  put out the flame
That they light in His name? See, the pyre
  is aflame!

Dieu souffre ces forfaits! Dieu n'éteint pas
  ces flammes!
Et l'on dresse en son nom ces bûchers tout
  en feu!

PHILIP, THE MONKS, THE PEOPLE

Praise to God!

Gloire à Dieu!

The flames of the pyre rise up.

Guardie, disarmato!
Ei sia. Signor, sostegni del mio trono,
Disarmato ei sia! Ma che? Nessuno?

Or ben, di voi chi l'oserà?
A quest'acciar chi sfuggirà?

Disarmato ei sia!

A me il ferro!

        O ciel!

             Tu! Rodrigo!

                    Egli! Posa!

Ei!

Marchese, Duca siete . . . Andiamo or alla
festa!

Volate verso il ciel, volate, povere alme,

V'affrettate a goder la pace del Signor!

Sì, la pace!

E puoi soffrirlo, o ciel! Né spegni quelle
fiamme!
S'accende in nome tuo quel rogo punitor!
E in nome del Signor l'accende l'oppressor!

Gloria al ciel!

The 'auto-da-fé', Cologne, 1964 (photo:
Gerd Preser)

Act Four *

Scene One. *The King's study.*

Scena and Cantabile of Philip. [16]

Philip, plunged in a profound reverie, is leaning on a table covered in papers, where the tapers are spent. Day begins to lighten the window-panes.

PHILIP *as if in a dream*

She has no love for me! No! She closes her heart,	Elle ne m'aime pas! non! son coeur m'est fermé,
She has no love for me!	Elle ne m'a jamais aimé!
Well I recall her glance when she met me in silence,	Je la revois encor, regardant en silence
Saw my grey hair, that day she came from France to wed me.	Mes cheveux blancs, le jour qu'elle arriva de France.
No! She has no love for me!	Non, elle ne m'aime pas!
coming to	
Where am I? All the candles	Où suis-je? Ces flambeaux
Are burnt out . . . The silver dawn is in the sky,	Sont consumés . . . L'aurore argente ces vitraux,
And it is day! Alas! Gentle sleep that could calm me	Voici le jour! Hélas! Le sommeil salutaire,
Forever has fled from my weary eyes!	Le doux sommeil a fui pour jamais ma paupière!
I'll only sleep when I am laid to rest, wrapped in royal robes,	Je dormirai dans mon manteau royal,
When my last hour has called me.	Quand aura lieu pour moi l'heure dernière, §
Then I shall sleep in a cold tomb of marble,	[17] Je dormirai sous les voûtes de pierre,
In the vaults of the Escorial!	Des caveaux de l'Escurial!

[16] ACT FOUR - Scena and Cantabile

[17] PHILIP

* Act Three in the four-act Milan version. According to the Paris score, this is in Valladolid but according to the Italian versions it is in Madrid. The Escorial was, of course, not built in 1559 when the action of the opera is supposed to take place.

Ella giammai m'amò! No, quel cor chiuso m'è.
Amor per me non ha!
Io la rivedo ancor contemplar triste in volto

Il mio crin bianco il dì che qui di Francia venne.
No, amor per me non ha!

Ove son? . . . Quei doppier
Presso a finir! . . . L'aurora imbianca il mio veron!
Già spunta il dì! Passar veggo i miei giorni lenti!
Il sonno, oh Dio! sparì da' miei occhi languenti!

Dormirò sol nel manto mio regal

Quando la mia giornata è giunta a sera;

§ Quand sonnera pour moi l'heure dernière,

Dormirò sol sotto la volta nera,

Là, nell'avello dell'Escurial.

-rai sous les voû - - tes de pier - re des ca - veaux — de l'Es-cu-ri - al!
sot - to la vol - - ta ne - ra là nel-l'a-vel - lo del-l'Es-cu-ri - al.
-cure in a cold_____ tomb of mar - ble in the vaults of the Es-cu-ri - al.

pp

Ah! Why can the crown not bestow on me the power
To read deep in men's hearts where God alone can see!
If the King sleeps, treachery stirs in the darkness,
Plotting to seize both his crown and his wife!

Ah! Why cannot the crown give to monarchs the power
To look into men's hearts!
She has no love for me! No! She closes her heart!
She has no love for me!

He falls back into his reverie.

Scena: the King and the Inquisitor.

THE COUNT OF LERMA *entering*

The Grand Inquisitor!

Lerma leaves. The Grand Inquisitor, blind, ninety years old, enters, supported by two monks. [18]

THE INQUISITOR ◊

Am I before the King?

PHILIP

Yes, I have sent for you, my father. I need your help.
The Prince disturbs my peace, fills all my days with sorrow.
My son has drawn his sword against his own father.

THE INQUISITOR

And what have you decided to do?

PHILIP

All . . . or nothing!

THE INQUISITOR

Explain your words!

PHILIP

Into exile . . . or else the scaffold . . .

Ah! Si la royauté nous donnait le pouvoir

De lire au fond des coeurs où Dieu seul peut tout voir!
Si le Roi dort, la trahison se trame, §

On lui ravit sa couronne et sa femme!

Ah! Si la royauté nous donnait le pouvoir
De lire au fond des coeurs!
Elle ne m'aime pas! non! son coeur m'est fermé.
Elle ne m'aime pas!

Le Grand Inquisiteur!

Suis-je devant le Roi?

Oui, j'ai recours à vous, mon père, éclairez-moi.
L'Infant remplit mon coeur d'une tristesse amère,
L'Infant est un rebelle armé contre son père.

Qu'avez-vous décidé contre lui?

Tout . . . ou rien!

Expliquez-vous!

Qu'il fuie . . . ou que le glaive . . .

---

[18] The Entrance of the Grand Inquisitor

Se il serto regal a me desse il poter

Di leggere nei cor, che Dio può sol
   veder! . . .
Se dorme il prence, veglia il traditore;

Il serto perde il Re, il consorte l'onore!

Ah! se il serto regal a me desse il poter

Di leggere nei cor!
Ella giammai m'amò! No, quel cor chiuso
   m'è.
Amor per me non ha!

§ Si le Roi dort, dans l'ombre on trame
Mille complots mystérieux
Et si l'époux ferme un instant ses yeux,
C'en est fait de l'honneur de sa femme!

Il Grande Inquisitor!

◊ According to the *Disposizione Scenica*,
the Grand Inquisitor is 'a blind, ninety-
year-old man — imposing, full of the
exalted task entrusted to him by God.'

Son io dinanzi al Re?

Sì, vi feci chiamar, mio padre! In dubbio io
   son.
Carlo mi colma il cor d'una tristezza
   amara.
L'Infant'è a me ribelle, armossi contro il
   padre.

Qual mezzo per punir scegli tu?

Mezzo estrem.

Noto mi sia!

Che fugga . . . o che la scure . . .

*Diagram from the 'Disposizione Scenica' for
the King's study. As the curtain rises Philip
is seated in a large armchair, sunk in
profound meditation, and leaning on a table
cluttered with papers, where two two-
branched candlesticks, with candles which
are almost spent. Elisabeth enters from A.
When she swoons, Philip runs to A, and
Eboli rushes in to help Elisabeth; Philip
makes to leave by B where he meets Rodrigo,
and they both return centre stage.*

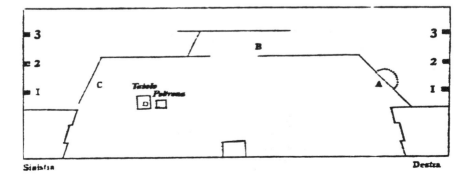

THE INQUISITOR

And then?   Eh bien?

PHILIP

If I put him to death, will you give me   Si je frappe l'Infant, ta main m'absoudrait-
absolution?   elle?

THE INQUISITOR

The peace of this empire demands the   La paix du monde vaut le sang d'un fils
blood of sons in rebellion.   rebelle.

PHILIP

How can I kill my son for the empire, I,   Puis-je immoler mon fils au monde, moi
a Christian?   chrétien?

THE INQUISITOR

God, to save the world, sacrificed His only   Dieu, pour nous sauver tous, sacrifia le
son.   sien.

PHILIP

Can you impose on all such a faith, harsh   Peux-tu fonder partout une foi si sévère?
and cruel?

THE INQUISITOR

On all, wherever the Cross has been raised   Partout où le chrétien suit la foi du Calvaire.
to inspire them.

PHILIP

What of nature and love? May I not   La nature et le sang se tairont-ils en moi?
heed their voice?

THE INQUISITOR

Human feelings must die when the   Tout s'incline et se tait lorsque parle la foi!
Church gives command!

PHILIP

So be it!   C'est bien!

THE INQUISITOR

And has the King nothing else he   Philippe Deux n'a plus rien à me dire?
must tell me?

PHILIP

No!   Non!

THE INQUISITOR

Then I, I must speak to you!   C'est donc moi qui vous parlerai, Sire!

In this land of Spain, no heresy has   Dans ce beau pays, pur d'hérétique levain,
thrived,
But now a man has dared undermine Holy   Un homme ose saper l'édifice divin.
Church.
He's friendly with the King, shares in   Il est l'ami du Roi, son confident intime,
his secret counsels,
He's a fiend who is driving the King to   Le démon tentateur qui le pousse à
destruction!   l'abîme,
For the crimes of the Prince, which   Les desseins criminels dont vous chargez
cause you such distress,   l'Infant
Compared to his are naught but the games   Ne sont auprès des siens que les jeux d'un
of a child.   enfant;
And I, your Grand Inquisitor, while   Et moi, l'Inquisiteur, moi, pendant que
raising my hand   je lève
On the poor and the weak, condemning   Sur d'obscurs criminels la main qui tient
them to die,   le glaive,

Ebben?

Se il figlio a morte invio, m'assolve la tua
mano?

La pace dell'impero i dì val d'un ribelle.

Posso il figlio immolar al mondo, io
cristian?

Per riscattarci Iddio il suo sacrificò.

Ma tu puoi dar vigor a legge sì severa?

Ovunque avrà vigor, se sul Calvario l'ebbe.

La natura, l'amor tacer potranno in me?

Tutto tacer dovrà per esaltar la fě.

Sta ben.

Non vuol il Re su d'altro interrogarmi?

No.

Allor son io ch'a voi parlerò, Sire.
Nell'ispano suol mai l'eresia dominò,

Ma v'ha chi vuol minar l'edifizio divin.

L'amico egli è del Re, il suo fedel compagno,

Il demon tentator che lo spinge a rovina.

Di Carlo il tradimento che giunse a
t'irritar,
In paragon del suo futile gioco appar.

Ed io, l'Inquisitor, io che levai sovente

Sopra orde vil di rei la mano mia possente,

*Barseg Tumanyan as Philip, Los Angeles
Music Center Opera, 1990 (photo: Frederic
Ohringer)*

I have withheld my sword from the great
  ones of this land,
I've left in peace so far this evil traitor . . .
  and you!

PHILIP

I sought an honest man to share my heavy
  burdens.
I had need of a friend among my band
  of courtiers,
A man, a trusted friend . . . and he was
  found!

THE INQUISITOR

          You sought a friend.
Then by what right can you be called
  a King,
Highness, if you have need of a friend?

PHILIP

          Hold your tongue, priest!

THE INQUISITOR

The spirit of reform has poisoned you
  already!
Do you think that your feeble hand can
  ever shake
That holy yoke that the Church has laid on
  all your world!
Return, King, to your duty! The Church, a
  kindly mother,
Will forgive erring sons when their
  repentance is sincere.
You must yield us the Marquis of Posa!

PHILIP

          No, by God!

THE INQUISITOR

O King, were I not here with you,
By my God, I swear, before my Court the
  King himself
Would be made to stand before the
  Inquisition!

PHILIP

Priest! For far too long I have borne with
  your pride!

THE INQUISITOR

Then why did you evoke the shade of
  Samuel?
I taught you in your youth. Two kings I've
  given this empire.
Must now the work of my days be destroyed
  by your madness!
Then why was I called here? Of me, what
  do you ask?

He prepares to leave.

PHILIP

My father, may the peace we have known
  be restored.

Pour les puissants du monde abjurant mon
  courroux,
Je laisse vivre en paix ce grand coupable . . .
  et vous!

Pour traverser les jours d'épreuves où nous
  sommes,
J'ai cherché dans ma cour, ce vaste désert
  d'hommes,
Un homme, un ami sûr . . . Je l'ai trouvé!

          Pourquoi
Un homme? Et de quel droit vous
  nommez-vous le Roi,
Sire, si vous avez des égaux?

          Tais-toi, prêtre!

L'esprit des novateurs chez vous déjà
  pénètre!
Vous voulez secouer de votre faible main

Le saint joug étendu sur l'univers romain!

Rentrez dans le devoir! L'Eglise, en bonne
  mère,
Peut encore accueillir un repentir sincère.

Livrez-nous le marquis de Posa!

          Non, jamais?

O Roi, si je n'étais ici, dans ce palais
Aujourd'hui: par le Dieu vivant, demain
  vous-même,
Vous seriez devant nous au tribunal
  suprême!

Prêtre! J'ai trop souffert ton orgueil
  criminel!

Pourquoi l'évoquiez-vous, l'ombre de
  Samuel?
J'avais donné deux rois à ce puissant empire,

L'oeuvre de tous mes jours, vous voulez
  la détruire . . .
Que viens-je faire ici? De moi que
  vouliez-vous?

Mon père, que la paix redescende entre
  nous.

Pei grandi di quaggiù, scordando la mia fé

Tranquilli lascio andar un gran ribelle . . . e
    il Re!

Per traversar i dì dolenti in cui viviamo

Nella mia corte invan cercat'ho quel che
    bramo,
Un uomo! Un cor leal! . . . Io lo trovai!

                                Perché
Un uomo? Perché allor il nome hai
    tu di Re,
Sire, s'alcun v'ha pari a te?

                    Non più, frate!

Le idee dei novator in te son penetrate!

Infrangere tu vuoi con la tua debol man

Il santo giogo, esteso sovra l'orbe roman!

Ritorna al tuo dover! La Chiesa all'uom che
    spera,
A chi si pente, puote offrir la venia intera;

A te chiedo il signor di Posa.

                        No, giammai!

O Re, se non foss'io con te nel regio ostel
Oggi stesso, lo giuro a Dio, doman saresti

Presso il Grande Inquisitor al tribunal
    supremo.

Frate! Troppo soffrii il tuo parlar crudel!

Perché evocar allor l'ombra di Samuel?

Dato ho finor due Regi al regno tuo
    possente!
L'opra di tanti dì tu vuoi strugger,
    demente! . . .
Perché mi trovo io qui? Che vuol il Re da
    me?

Mio padre, che tra noi la pace alberghi
    ancor.

*Hans Hotter as the Grand Inquisitor,
Metropolitan Opera, 1958 (photo:
Metropolitan Opera Archive)*

THE INQUISITOR *continuing to move away*

What peace?

La paix?

PHILIP

   Can you forget all that has passed?

Que le passé soit oublié!

THE INQUISITOR *on the threshold, as he leaves*

          It may be!

          Peut-être!

PHILIP

The King himself is humbled when the priest commands him!

L'orgueil du Roi fléchit devant l'orgueil du prêtre!

Scena and Quartet.

ELISABETH *entering and throwing herself at the King's feet* *

I come here to ask for justice!
I look to you to redress my wrongs!

Justice! Sire! J'ai foi
Dans la loyauté du Roi!

For here at Court, unworthily and shamefully I'm scorned,
And by some secret foe I am wronged and insulted . . .

Je suis dans votre court indignement traitée
Et par des ennemis inconnus insultée.

For a casket that contains, Sire, the things I value,
All my jewels . . . not only them, but all I hold most dear . . .
A thief has dared to steal! I ask you for justice!
I demand that the King redress my wrongs!

Mon coffret . . . il contient, Sire, tout un trésor,
Mes bijoux . . . des objets plus précieux encor . . .
On l'a volé! chez moi! Justice! je réclame
De Votre Majesté!

As she perceives the terrible expression on Philip's face, Elisabeth breaks off, alarmed. The King rises slowly, takes a casket from the table, and offers it to the Queen.

PHILIP

         Those gems you seek, my lady,
Here they are!

         Votre coffret, Madame,

Le voilà!

ELISABETH

      Heaven!

      Ciel!

PHILIP

        Will you open it and see?
Elisabeth makes a gesture of refusal.
I'll open it myself!
forcing the casket

         Vous plaît-il de l'ouvrir?

Je l'ouvrirai donc, moi!

ELISABETH

      Heaven! What can save me now?

      Dieu! viens me secourir!

PHILIP

Here's a portrait of Carlos!

Un portrait de l'Infant!

ELISABETH

      Yes!

      Oui!

PHILIP

      Concealed with your jewels?

      Parmi vos bijoux?

ELISABETH

Yes!

Oui!

PHILIP

What! You dare confess that to me?

Quoi! Vous l'avouez devant moi!

112

La pace?

Obliar tu dêi quel ch'è passato.

Forse!

Dunque il trono piegar dovrà sempre
all'altare!

Giustizia! Sire. Ho fé
Nella lealtà del Re!
Son nella corte tua crudelmente trattata

E da nemici oscuri, incogniti, oltraggiata.

Lo scrigno ov'io chiudea, Sire, tutt'un tesor,

I gioielli . . . altri oggetti a me più cari
    ancor . . .
L'hanno rapito a me! . . . Giustizia! la
    reclamo
Dal potere del Re!

*Cesare Siepi (Philip) and Hermann Uhde
(Grand Inquisitor), Metropolitan Opera,
1958 (photo: Metropolitan Opera Archive)*

Quello che voi cercate,
Eccolo!

* This passage, through to the end of
the scene, was musically revised for
Milan (though in the early part, the
words remain the same as those in the
original version).

Ciel!

A voi d'aprirlo piaccia.

Ebben, io l'aprirò.

(Ah! mi sento morir!)

Il ritratto di Carlo! †

† See appendix for the revised text of
the Milan version.

Sì!

Misto ai vostri gioiel?

Sì!

Che! Confessar l'osate a me!

113

ELISABETH

Yes, I dare!
This portrait, I had it in France.
When God made me your husband,
I was betrothed to the Infante!
How can I banish from my thoughts
The bond that united us?
For Carlos I feel a mother's care.
If God deigns to hear me, one day
The Infante will receive from his father
More justice, and more love!

PHILIP

You're far too bold, you speak too freely!
So far you've only known me in my
moments of weakness.
That weakness will not last; you'll see it
turn to rage.
And then, beware! Beware!

ELISABETH

And what has been my crime?

PHILIP

You lied to me!
If your disgrace is as deep as I think it,
If you've betrayed me . . . then by God
high above,
I swear to be revenged with blood!

ELISABETH

How I pity you!

PHILIP

You dare pity me? An adulterous wife!

ELISABETH *swooning*

Ah!

PHILIP *opening the doors*

Come and help the Queen!

Eboli enters hastily, Rodrigo a little later.

EBOLI *alarmed as she sees the Queen in a swoon*

(Ah! What have I done? Alas!)

RODRIGO *to Philip*

Sire! . . . When half of this world looks to
you as its ruler,
One man alone you have failed to
subdue!
The King has no power to command
himself?

PHILIP

(Accurst be this hour, o unworthy
suspicion,
Work of a cruel fiend sent from Hell!

Devant vous!
Ce portrait, je l'avais en France.
Lorsque Dieu vous fit mon époux,
A l'Infant j'étais fiancée!
Comment chasser de ma pensée
Le lien qui fut entre nous?
J'ai pour Carlos un coeur de mère.
Si Dieu daigne m'entendre, un jour
L'Infant trouvera chez son père
Plus de justice et plus d'amour!

Vous me parlez avec hardiesse!
Vous ne m'avez connu . . . qu'en des jours
de faiblesse; §
Mais la faiblesse un jour peut devenir fureur.

Alors, malheur sur vous, sur vous!

Quel crime ai-je commis?

Parjure!
Si l'infamie a comblé la mesure,
Si vous m'avez trahi . . . par le Dieu tout
puissant,
Tremblez! Je verserai le sang!

Je vous plains!

Vous! Me plaindre? Une femme adultère! §§

Ah!

Secourez la Reine!

(Oh, ciel! Que vois-je? Hélas!)

Sire! . . . A vous obéit la moitié de la terre:
Etes-vous donc, dans vos vastes Etats,
Le seul à qui vous ne commandiez pas?

(Maudit soit le soupçon infâme,

Oeuvre d'un démon odieux!

                        Perchè negarlo?
Quel ritratto in Francia io l'ebbi.

Quando Dio mi fe' tua sposa,
Ero a Carlo fidanzata!
Ma la fede a te giurata
Non tradiva questo cor.
Ho per lui l'amor di madre.
Se il ciel ode il voto mio,
Trovar Carlo può nel padre
Più clemenza e men rigor!

Ardita troppo voi favellate!
Me debole credete e sfidarmi sembrate:

La debolezza in me può divenir furor.

Tremate allor per voi, per me.

Qual colpa è in me?

                        Spergiura!
Se il fallo tuo colmò la misura,
Se tradito son io, sì, lo giuro innanzi al
    ciel.
Il sangue verserò!

Pietà mi fate.

            Ah! la pietà d'adultera consorte!

Ah!

Aita alla Regina!

(Oh, Ciel! Che veggo?! Ahimè!)

Sire! . . . obedisce a voi una metà del mondo:

Sareste dunque in così vasto regno

Il solo a cui non commandiate voi?

(Ah! sia maledetto, il rio sospetto,

che sol l'inferno in me destò!

§ Vous m'avez connu faible et me
bravez en face.

§§ La pitiè d'une femme adultère!

*Maria Chiara (Elisabeth) and Simon Estes
(Philip), Opernhaus-Zurich, 1979 (photo:
Susan Schimert-Ramme)*

115

No! She is proud and she is honest,
I know her soul is pure and true!

† Non! La fierté de cette femme
N'est pas le crime audacieux!)

RODRIGO

(The time has come, I hear the thunder,
The lightning flashes and I must act.
This land of Spain requires a victim,
Who will die to ensure future peace!
Who will die to ensure future peace!)

(Il faut agir et voici l'heure.
La foudre gronde au sein des cieux.
Que pour l'Espagne un homme meure,
En lui léguant des jours heureux,
En lui léguant l'avenir radieux!)

EBOLI

(O remorse! O regret unavailing!
I have sinned, committed a crime, o
remorse!
Ah! I've betrayed my innocent Queen!
How can I hope now for peace?)

(O remords, amère tristesse! §
Que mon pardon vienne des cieux!

J'ai trahi ma noble maîtresse,
J'ai commis un crime odieux!)

ELISABETH *coming to*

Where am I? Alas! Ah, see me, mother!
See these tears that burn in my eyes.
Alone in this country so unfriendly!
Grant, oh God, grant me peace!

Où suis-je? Hélas! Ma pauvre mère, §§
Vois les pleurs qui brûlent mes yeux.
Je suis sur la terre étrangère!
Mon seul espoir est dans les cieux.

The King, after a moment of hesitation, leaves. Rodrigo makes a decisive gesture and follows him. Eboli remains alone with the Queen.

Scena and Aria.

*

EBOLI *throwing herself at Elisabeth's feet*

Forgive and pardon a woman who's
wronged you!

Pitié! Pardon pour la femme coupable!

ELISABETH

Why do you kneel? What is it?

Relevez-vous! Quel crime? . . .

EBOLI

       Ah! My remorse overwhelms me!
My heart will break with grief!
Angel from Heaven, o my Queen true and
noble,
Now learn what cruel fiend from Hell has
worked your ruin!
Your case of jewels was stolen by me!

       Ah! Le remords m'accable!
Mon coeur est désolé.
Ange du ciel, Reine auguste et sacrée,

Sachez à quel démon l'enfer vous a livrée!

Votre coffret . . . c'est moi qui l'ai volé!

ELISABETH

You!

Vous! §§§

EBOLI

   Yes, I it was accused you!

Oui, par moi vous fûtes accusée!

ELISABETH

What, you!

Par vous!

[19] PHILIP

Largo
cantabile

Non!	la fier-té	de cet	-	te fem	- me n'est pas	le
No!	non mac-chiò	la fe'		giu - ra	- ta,	a me in - fe -
No!	she is proud,	she's proud	and hon-est, I	know that	her	

116

No, non macchiò la fé giurata,
Esser infida costei non può!)

(Ormai d'oprar suonata è l'ora,
Folgore orrenda in ciel brillò!
Che per la Spagna un uomo mora . . .
Lieto avvenir le lascerò,
Lieto avvenir le lascerò!)

(Io la perdei! Tristezza amara!
Il fallo mio la condannò!

La mia Regina a me sì cara,
Io la tradii! Ah, ne morrò!)

Che avvenne! O ciel! in pianto, in duolo
Ognun, o madre, m'abbandonò,
Sola, straniera in questo suolo,
Più sulla terra speme non ho.

Pietà! perdon! per la rea che si pente.

Al mio piè! Voi! Qual colpa?

               Ah! m'uccide il rimorso!
Torturato è il mio cor.
Angel del ciel, Regina augusta e pia,

Sappiate a qual demòn l'inferno vi dà in
   preda;
Quello scrigno . . . son io che l'involai.

Voi!

Sì, son io, son io che v'accusai!

Voi!

† Music example [19] gives the Milan
version of the quartet (see p. 151).

§ O remords! amère tristresse!
J'ai commis un crime odieux,
J'ai trahi ma noble maîtresse;
Mon pardon viendra-t-il des cieux?

§§ Viens ici, viens ma pauvre mère,

* This passage was cut before the Paris
première in 1867 (see note on p. 121 for
the end of the cut). Instead of the
Queen's forgiving Eboli her love of
Carlos and only turning from her when
Eboli reveals that she has been seduced
by the King, the cut means that
Elisabeth appears to reject Eboli
because of the latter's love for Carlos.
No mention is made of her relationship
with the King. This reduces both the
drama of the scene and the force of
Eboli's inveighing against her beauty.
Unless that relationship is made clear,
Elisabeth's reaction seems irrationally
harsh. In the cut version given in Paris
in 1867, Eboli is consigned to choose
between exile and the convent by
Elisabeth, rather than by the Count of
Lerma, and it is that version which
appears in the printed libretto.

§§§
EBOLI Oui, pour le Roi!
ELISABETH Vous!
EBOLI Pour vous perdre!
ELISABETH Insensée! Vous me haïssiez
  donc?

cri	-	-	me, _____	le	cri - me au-da - ci -	eux!
-de	-	-	le, _____	in -	fe - de - le	non	fu.
soul __	is	pure, _____	that	her soul __	is	true.

EBOLI

Yes, my love and my rage, the hate I felt for you!
Passion and fury combined to torment me and jealousy poisoned my heart!
I loved Don Carlos ... by him I was rejected!

Oui! L'amour, la fureur, ma haine contre vous!
Tous les tourments jaloux déchaînés dans mon coeur.
J'aimais l'Infant ... l'Infant m'a repoussée!

ELISABETH *

[I have understood all ... to my amazed eye
The fearful plot is revealed ...
But I feel sorry for the wretched pain
Of this heart condemned to remorse.]

J'ai tout compris ... à mon oeil étonné
Se montre la trame effroyable ...
Mais de ce coeur au remords condamné,
Je plains la douleur misérable.

EBOLI

[Dreadful remorse, hell with avenging fire,
Burns my wretched soul,
And nothing can ever end the horror
Of this dreadful torture.]

L'affreux remords, enfer au feu vengeur
Brûle mon âme misérable,
Et rien jamais ne finira l'horreur
De cette torture effroyable.

ELISABETH

[(Ah! May Heaven pardon
Her bitter regrets,
May its goodness give her
Hope and peace!)]

(Ah! Que le ciel pardonne
A ses amers regrets,
Que sa bonté lui donne
L'espérance et la paix!)

EBOLI

[My broken heart shudders
With grief, with regrets,
God never pardons
Such crimes.]

Mon coeur brisé frissonne
De douleur, de regrets,
Dieu jamais ne pardonne
A de pareils forfaits.

She falls to her knees.

ELISABETH

[You loved him? Rise ... I have already forgiven!]

Vous l'aimiez? Levez-vous ... j'ai déjà pardonné!

EBOLI

[No forgiveness! Another terrible confession.]

Point de pardon! Encore un aveu terrible.

ELISABETH

[Another?]

Encor?

EBOLI

[The unforgivable crime
Of which I accused you, I committed it, I ...
A seduction ... the King!]

Le crime irrémissible
Dont je vous accusais, je l'avais commis, moi ...
Une séduction ... le Roi!

ELISABETH

[(Horror!)]

(Horreur!)

She covers her face and leaves without speaking.

EBOLI

[She has condemned me!
All is over, I am abandoned by Heaven!]

Elle m'a condamnée!
Tout est fini, je suis du ciel abandonnée!

COUNT LERMA *entering*

Princess, return me your cross!

Princesse, rendez-moi votre croix!

118

Sì . . . l'amor, il furor, l'odio che avea per
    voi . . .
La gelosia crudel che straziavami il cor
    contro voi m'eccitar.
Io Carlo amavo, e Carlo mi sprezzò!

Or tutto è chiaro! Al mio occhio
    sgomento
Appare la trama delittuosa,
Ma di costei che per lui si dannò,
Io piango il dolor spaventoso!

* The English text in square brackets is
a literal translation.

L'atroce rimorso, inferno punitor,
Brucia quest'alma ch'è sì peccaminosa
E nulla ormai può cancellar l'orror
Dì questa tortura spaventosa.

(Ah! Che il ciel perdoni
À lei ch'è già punita dal dolor,
Che in sua bontà le doni
La speranza e l'amor!)

Il cuor spezzato trema
Di rimorso e dolor,
Dio non può perdonare
A tanto disonor.

Voi l'amaste . . . Vi rialzate io v'ho già
    perdonata!

No, non ancor! Ho un'altra colpa orribil.

Un'altra?

        La colpa irremissibil
Di cui io v'accusai . . . commessa fu da
    me . . .
Una seduzione . . . il Re!

(Orror!)

        Lei m'ha condannata!
Tutto finì, io son dal ciel abbandonata!

Principessa, date a me la vostra croce!

*Margaret Price as Elisabeth, Teatro Lírico
Nacional La Zarzuela, Madrid (photo:
Antonio de Benito)*

119

EBOLI *obediently, trembling*

Shall I see My noble Queen again?	Se peut-il Que je revoie encor ma noble souveraine?

COUNT LERMA

Before tomorrow's dawn you shall choose Between a convent and exile. Live happy!	Vous choisirez avant l'aube prochaine, Entre un cloître et l'exil. Vivez heureuse! *

EBOLI *alone*

Ah! Shall I never see her again!	Ah! Je ne verrai plus la Reine!
My beauty dooms me, o fatal gift, That Heaven bestowed in anger! My beauty made me so cruel and proud! Vainly I curse its fatal power!	O don fatal et détesté. Présent du ciel en sa colère! O toi qui rends la femme si fière, Je te maudis, ô ma beauté!
Although my bitter tears are flowing, They cannot wash away my grief, My repentance, my cruel anguish, Cannot change what I've done or bring relief!	Tombez, tombez, larmes amères! Mes trahisons et mes forfaits, Mes souillures et mes misères, Vous ne les laverez jamais!
Vainly I curse my beauty's power!	Je te maudis, ô ma beauté!
Queen, I wronged you, fallen a victim, To my furious passions and my foolish love! Far from the world, in some lonely cloister, [20] I shall take the veil, and be lost evermore!	Adieu, Reine, victime pure De mes déloyales et folles amours! Dans un couvent et sous la bure, Je m'ensevelis pour toujours!
And Carlos! Ah! Perhaps tomorrow, The Prince will fall to the holy sword! Ah! One day is left me! And hope once more revives me! I bless that day . . . I shall save him!	Et Carlos? . . . Oui! demain, peut-être, Il tombera sous le fer sacré! Ah! Un jour me reste! Ah! Je me sens renaître! Béni ce jour . . . Je le sauverai!

She leaves abruptly.

Scene Two. *Don Carlos' prison. A crypt into which some fine furniture has been hastily thrown. At the back, iron grilles divide the prison from the courtyard above, where guards pass to and fro; a flight of stone steps leads down into the courtyard from the upper storeys of the palace. Don Carlos is seated, his head in his hands. Rodrigo enters, talks quietly to some officers. He makes a move that rouses Don Carlos from his reverie.*

Scena and Aria of Posa.

RODRIGO

I'm here, my Carlos!	C'est moi, Carlos!

DON CARLOS *giving him his hand*

My Rodrigo, my only friend! You've come to see me here in this my tomb!	Mon Rodrigue! Il est beau A toi de me venir trouver dans ce tombeau!

RODRIGO

Carlos!	Carlos!

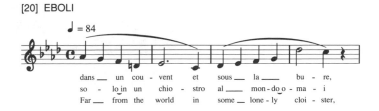

[20] EBOLI

♩ = 84

dans __ un cou - vent   et   sous __ la ___ bu - re,
so - lo in un   chio - stro   al ___ mon - do o - ma - i
Far __ from the   world   in   some __ lone - ly   cloi - ster,

120

            Potrò mai
La nobil mia sovrana io riveder ancora?

Dato vi fia pria della nuova aurora,
Sceglier l'esilio o il vel.
Siate felice!

* The end of the passage which Verdi rewrote for the first performance in Paris.

          Ah! più non vedrò la Regina!

O don fatale, o don crudel,
Che in suo furor mi fece il cielo!
Tu che ci fai sì vane, altere,
Ti maledico, o mia beltà.

Versar, versar sol posso il pianto,
Speme non ho, soffrir dovrò!
Il mio delitto è orribil tanto
Che cancellar mai nol potrò!

Ti maledico, ti maledico, o mia beltà!

O mia Regina, io t'immolai
Al folle error, di questo cor.
Solo in un chiostro al mondo omai
Dovrò celar il mio dolor!

O Ciel! E Carlo? a morte domani,
Gran Dio! a morte andar vedrò!
Ah! un dì mi resta, la speme m'arride!

Sia benedetto il ciel! Lo salverò!

Son io, mio Carlo.

        O Rodrigo, io ti son
Ben grato di venir di Carlo alla prigion.

Giorgio Zancanaro (Rodrigo) and Luis Lima (Don Carlos), Opernhaus-Zurich, 1979 (photo: Susan Schimert-Ramme)

Mio Carlo!

dans _ un _ cou - vent ____   et ____ sous _ la bu - re!
do - vrò _ ce - lar ____   il ____ mi - o do - lo - re!
I'll _ take _ the veil, ____   in _ some lone-ly cloi - ster!

121

DON CARLOS

You understand, that all my strength has failed me!
My love for Elisabeth tortures and kills me . . .
No! I can do no more for our Flanders! But you,
You can bring her that golden age we both longed to see!

Tu l'as compris, ma force est abattue!

L'amour d'Elisabeth me torture et me tue . . .
Non! Je ne puis plus rien pour les hommes! Mais toi,
Donne-leur les jours d'or qu'ils attendaient de moi!

RODRIGO

Ah! You have still to learn what love I bear you.
You soon will leave this gloomy place of death.
With loving tender pride let your friend now embrace you!
I've saved your life!

Ah! Connais mieux mon âme et ma tendresse.
Tu vas sortir de ce funèbre lieu.

Avec quel doux orgueil sur mon coeur je te presse!
Je t'ai sauvé!

DON CARLOS

My life?

Comment?

RODRIGO

And I must leave you; we say our last farewell!

Il faut nous dire adieu!

Don Carlos stands motionless, looking at Rodrigo with amazement.

O my Carlos, yes! My last day has dawned [21] Oui, Carlos! C'est mon jour suprême, forever,
You and I must now say goodbye.
Till that day when God unites us,
Till we meet once more on high!
In your eyes tears of grief are shining;
Why this glance of dread?
Dry those tears, for death is welcome,
O my Carlos, when I die for you!

Echangeons l'adieu solonnel.
Dieu permet encor qu'on s'aime
Près de lui, quand on est au ciel.
Dans tes yeux tout baignés de larmes,
Pourquoi donc ce muet effroi?
Qui plains-tu? La mort a des charmes,
O mon Carlos, à qui meurt pour toi!

DON CARLOS *trembling*

But why do you speak of death?

Que parles-tu de mort?

[21] RODRIGO

Andante sostenuto

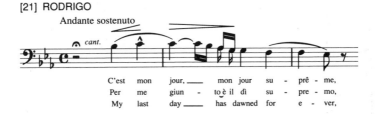

C'est mon jour, ___ mon jour su - prê - me,
Per me giun - to è il dì su - pre - mo,
My last day ___ has dawned for e - ver,

122

Ben tu il sai! m'abbandonò il vigore!

D'Elisabetta l'amor mi tortura e
   m'uccide . . .
No, più valor non ho pei viventi! Ma tu,

Puoi salvarli ancor; oppressi non fian più.

Ah! noto appien ti sia l'affetto mio!

Uscir tu dêi da quest'orrendo avel.

Felice ancor io son se abbracciarti poss'io!

Io ti salvai!

    Che di'?

          Convien qui dirci addio!

O mio Carlo! Per me giunto è il dì
   supremo,
No, mai più ci rivedrem;
Cì congiunga Iddio nel ciel,
Ei che premia i suoi fedel.
Sul tuo ciglio il pianto io miro;
Lagrimar così, perché?
No, fa cor, l'estremo spiro
Lieto è a chi morrà per te.

Che parli tu di morte?

*Tito Gobbi as Rodrigo, Covent Garden,
1962 (photo: Houston Rogers, Theatre
Museum Collection)*

*Diagram in the 'Disposizione Scenica'
for Don Carlos' prison. 1: the backcloth;
I: a balcony by which staircase V may be
reached in view of the audience; F: a gate;
R: another practicable gate; G: steps;
O: a large gate of golden bars;
M: a courtyard; T: a door; A: a stone bench.*

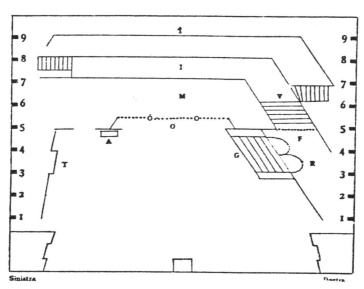

RODRIGO

Now hear me! Time is pressing . . .
For I have drawn on my head the
thunderbolt of vengeance!
And today it is not you they seek,
That man who stirs rebellion in Flanders . . .
is I!

Ecoute! Le temps presse . . .
J'ai détourné de toi la foudre vengeresse!
Aujourd'hui . . . le rival du Roi,
Le traitre agitateur de la Flandre . . . c'est
moi!

DON CARLOS

O my friend! Who'll believe it?

Malheureux! Qui croira?

RODRIGO

Twenty proofs attest it!
All your papers were found on me,
Plans and secret plots, overwhelming
proofs of treason . . .
A price is on my head; I have not long to
live!

Vingt preuves amassées!
Tes papiers chez moi surpris,
Preuves de trahison qu'à dessein j'ai
laissées . . .
Ma tête en ce moment sans doute est mise à
prix!

Two men come down the stone steps of the prison. One of them is clad in the robe of the Inquisition, the other is armed with a musket. They stop and point out to one another Don Carlos and Rodrigo, who do not observe them.

DON CARLOS

I'll go before the King . . .

J'irai devant le Roi . . .

RODRIGO

You must live for our Flanders!
You must live for our glorious endeavour,
till you see our dream come true . . .
Till the golden age is revived and Carlos is
King . . .
Yes, you shall live and rule and I must die
for you!

Garde-toi pour la Flandre!
Garde-toi pour notre oeuvre, il la faudra
défendre . . .
Un nouvel âge d'or renaîtra sous ta loi,
Oui, tu devais régner, et moi mourir pour
toi!

The man with the musket aims at Rodrigo and fires.

DON CARLOS *horrified*

God! A shot! Aimed at whom?

Ciel! La mort! Pour qui donc?

RODRIGO *mortally wounded*

At me! . . .
The revenge of the King has not been slow
to strike me!

Pour moi! . . .
La vengeance du Roi ne se fait pas attendre!

He falls into the distraught Don Carlos' arms.

DON CARLOS

O God!

Grand Dieu!

RODRIGO

Carlos, now hear me . . . Your mother
Awaits you at San Yuste tomorrow;
She knows our plan! Ah! my senses
Are failing! . . . Give me your hand, my
Carlos . . .

Carlos, ećoute . . . Ta mère
T'attend à Saint-Just demain;
Elle sait tout! . . . Ah! La terre
Me manque . . . O Carlos! ta main . . .

Ah! I die contented,
For by my death I've saved your life . . .
Ruler of Spain, saviour of Flanders!
Carlos, farewell, ah! Don't forget!

Ah! je meurs l'âme joyeuse,
Car tu vis sauvé par moi . . .
Ah! je vois l'Espagne heureuse!
Adieu! Carlos, ah! souviens-toi!

You must live and rule,
And I must die for you!

Oui, tu devais régner,
Et moi mourir pour toi!

124

Ascolta, il tempo stringe,
Rivolta ho già su me la folgore tremenda!

Tu più non sei oggi il rival del Re . . .
Il fiero agitator delle Fiandre . . . son io!

Chi potrà prestar fé?

Le prove son tremende!
I fogli tuoi trovati in mio poter . . .
Della ribellion testimoni son chiari,

E questo capo al certo a prezzo è messo
  già.

Svelar vo' tutto al Re.

No, ti serba alla Fiandra,
Ti serba alla grand'opra, tu la dovrai
  compire.
Un nuovo secol d'ôr rinascer tu farai;

Regnare tu dovevi ed io morir per te.

Ciel! La morte! Per chi mai?

Per me!
Le vendetta del Re, tardare-non potea!

Gran Dio!

O Carlo, ascolta . . . La madre t'aspetta
A San Giusto doman; tutto ella sa . . .
Ah! la terra mi manca . . . Carlo mio,
A me porgi la man! . . .

Io morrò, ma lieto in core,
Che potei così serbar
Alla Spagna un salvatore!
Ah! . . . di me . . . no ti scordar!

Sì, regnare tu dovevi,
Ed io morir per te.

Plácido Domingo (Don Carlos) and Louis
Quilico (Rodrigo), Metropolitan Opera,
1983 (photo: Winnie Klotz)

Ah! My senses are failing... Your hand,
   my friend...
O Carlos! Saviour of Flanders!
Carlos, farewell, ah! Farewell!

Ah! La terre me manque... Carlos,
   ta main...
Carlos! Ah! Sauve la Flandre!
Adieu! Carlos, ah! Adieu!

He dies. Don Carlos falls on his body in despair.

Finale. *

Philip, his retinue, Grandees of Spain and Count Lerma enter. Don Carlos is kneeling beside Rodrigo's body.

PHILIP *to Don Carlos, after a silence*

My son, now your sword is restored you;
The man I trusted has deceived me,
But the traitor has met his fate!

Mon fils, reprenez votre épée;
Ma confiance fut trompée,
Mais le traître a subi son sort!

He opens his arms to Don Carlos.

Now come!

Venez!

DON CARLOS *in despair, leaning over Rodrigo's body*

   No, never! Your hands are stained
   with blood,
The noble blood of my friend whom you
   murdered!
God marks your brow with blood, the
   seal of Cain stands there!

   Arrière! De ce mort

Le sang a rejailli jusqu'à votre visage!

Dieu marque votre front du sceau de
   son courroux!

PHILIP

My son!

Mon fils!

DON CARLOS

   I no more am your son!
Among your henchmen, go search
Till you find a son in your own image!

   Vouz n'avez plus de fils!
Choisissez-vous
Parmi ceux des bourreaux un fils
   à votre image!

PHILIP *to his henchmen, wanting to leave*

Follow me!

Suivez-moi!

DON CARLOS *leaping up and violently barring his way*

You who thought you knew the human
   heart,
You must learn what true blood has been
   shed by your hand!
This man loved me, we were as brothers...
Our loving hearts were bound by bonds
   that God had tied;
And your favours he scorned, and he
   dared to defy you,
And for me he has died!

Connaisseur profond du coeur humain,

Vouz saurez quel sang pur a versé
   votre main!
Il m'aimait et nous étions frères...
Nos coeurs étaient liés par d'éternels
   serments;
Méprisant vos bienfaits, méprisant vos
   colères,
C'est pour moi qu'il est mort!

PHILIP

   O, my secret fear!

   Dieu! Mes pressentiments!

DON CARLOS

O King of murder and of bloodshed!
Find someone else to carry your
   treacherous crown,
When the hour of death has come
   for you!

O Roi de meurtre et d'épouvante!
Cherche qui portera ta couronne
   sanglante
Quand ta dernière heure aura lieu!

pointing to Rodrigo's corpse
My only throne is beside my friend!

Mes royaumes sont près de lui!

He throws himself once again upon Rodrigo's body.

Ah! la terra mi manca . . . la mano
   a me . . .
Ah! salva la Fiandra!
Carlo, addio, ah, ah!

* The 'Emeute'. 'Sommossa' or
'Insurrection': this scene was cut in
some Paris performances and rewritten
for the Milan version (see appendix).

Carlo, il brando ormai riprendi;
Io fui tratto nell'errore,
Scontò il fallo il traditor!

Deh! Vien!

      T'arretra! D'un fedel

Il sangue il viso tuo feralmente macchiò!

Dio la vendetta sua sul fronte tuo
   stampò!

O figlio!

      Non son più tuo figlio! Scegliere puoi
Tra' carnefici tuoi un figlio a te simile!

Mi seguite!

      Scrutator ti credi del cor umano,

Nè sai qual puro sangue ha versato
   la tua man!
Ei m'amò come fratello . . .
Sacro giuro legò questo mio cor;

I tuoi doni sprezzando, il furor tuo
   del pari,
E per me che morì!

            Ciel! Presentimenti miei!

O Re d'eccidio e di spavento!
Cerca chi cingerà quel serto insanguinato

Allor che la tua fine arriverà!

Presso di lui il soglio mio sarà!

*Mikhail Litmanow (Philip) and Axel
Wagner (Grand Inquisitor), Stadttheater
Bern, 1991 (photo: Eduard Rieben)*

127

PHILIP

Who'll give me back this man? My distress and my sorrow!
For he alone among so many victims,
Yes, this man alone was courageous and true,
I have broken a bond that God himself had tied!

I loved that man . . . In words of burning fire,
He showed me a world where all men were brave!
His soul was proud . . . his heart was pure and noble,
By me he was condemned to his dark, lonely grave!

Who'll give me back this man?

Qui me rendra ce mort? O funèbres abîmes!
Celui-là seul . . . parmi tant de victimes!
Un homme, un seul, un héros était né,
J'ai brisé cet appui que Dieu m'avait donné!

Oui, je l'aimais . . . Sa noble parole
A l'âme révélait un monde nouveau!

Cet homme fier . . . ce coeur de flamme,
C'est moi qui l'ait jeté dans l'horreur du tombeau!

Qui me rendra ce mort?

THE COURTIERS

In vain, in vain the rest of us are living,

Since he alone is trusted by the King!

What of us? Shall we all follow him to the grave?

Ah! C'est en vain que nous vivons encore.
Il nous ravit le coeur du Roi que le regret dévore!
Espagnols! Descendons dans la nuit du tombeau!

DON CARLOS

My only friend, let me share in your glory!
I must rule in that world which together we planned!
Inspire my heart, fire it with dreams of freedom,
Or in peace let me lie in your grave.

O mon ami, donne-moi ta grande âme,

Fais de moi le héros de ton monde nouveau!
Remplis mon coeur de la divine flamme,

Ou fais moi près de toi place dans le tombeau.

Remainder of the Finale.

THE COURTIERS

Ha! The alarm!

Ciel! Le tocsin!

COUNT LERMA

The people rebel! O Sire!
They threaten your life! The mob is seized with madness!
They've stormed the gates of the palace, and they cry
They've come to set Don Carlos free!

Rébellion! O Sire!
Sauvez vos jours! Le peuple est en délire!
Il a forcé le palais, triomphant,
Il vient pour délivrer l'Infant!

Rodrigo's body is carried off. Don Carlos follows it in despair.

ELISABETH *entering in distress*

Protect the King!
Sire! I tremble for your life!
Escape, we'll flee together!

Sauvez le Roi!
Sire! Je tremble pour Votre Majesté!
Fuyons ensemble!

THE PEOPLE *offstage, behind the doors at the rear*

To death all who dare to oppose us!
We strike, and we strike to kill!
Beware the people's furious might!

La mort à qui nous arrête!
Frappons sans pitié, sans peur!
Tremblez devant le peuple vengeur!

Chi rende a me quest'uom? O abissi
    crudeli,
Salvate lui dagl'error miei fatali!
Un uomo, un sol, un eroe era nato,

Ho distrutto l'aiuto che Dio m'avea
    donato!

Sì, io l'amai, il nobil suo pensiero

A me rivelava il mondo del futuro,

E quest'uomo fiero . . . quest'anima
    ch'ardeva,
Son io che lo gettai d'una tomba
    nell'orror!

Chi rende a me quest'uom?

Perché . . . perché . . . perché viviamo
    ancora . . .
Lui ci rapì il cuor del Re . . . distrutto
    dal rimorso!
O Spagnoli, scendiam in quel regno
    d'orror!

O amico mio . . . dona a me il tuo cuore,

Fa di me un eroe del pensier novator!

Infondi in me la tua divina fiamma

O richiamami a te in quel regno d'orror!

Ciel! Qual suon!

                    Ribellion! O Grandi,
Si salvi il Re! Il popolo s'insorge!

Le reggie porte atterrò,

Qui verrà per liberar l'Infante!

Salvate il Re!
Sire! Il cor trema per Vostra Maestà!
Fuggiam insieme!

Morte! Niun ci arresta!
Bando alfin al timor!
Tremi il Re, se tutto il popol sorge
    in furor!

* This section was cut before the first
Paris performance (see the next asterisk
for the end of the cut). Philip's music
was reworked by Verdi for the
'Lacrimosa' of his Requiem (1873/74).
It did not, therefore, feature in the
1883/84 Milan version.

*Boris Christoff as Philip (photo: Royal
Opera House Archives)*

PHILIP *with authority, indicating the doors at the rear, behind which the menacing crowd has already gathered*

Then let the doors be opened!   Ouvrez ces portes!

ELISABETH

Ah!   Ciel!

COUNT LERMA

The people are enraged!   Le peuple est furieux!

PHILIP

Let the doors be opened, I command!   Ouvrez ces portes! Je le veux!

COUNT LERMA

Grandees of Spain, protect the King!   Grands d'Espagne, sauvez le Roi!

THE GRANDEES OF SPAIN *sword in hand*

Death to the rebels! Long live the King!   Mort aux rebelles! Vive le Roi!

The People enter in a fury. § *Reprise of the Chorus.*

PHILIP *to the People*

Then strike! Do not delay! Here I am! Do not fear me!
Take my life, I am old, men who are loyal and true!
Then trample on my bleeding corpse, March on to render homage to Carlos, my son!
The treacherous son who seized his father's crown!

Frappez! Que tardez-vous? Me voilà! Du courage!
Egorgez un vieillard, hommes au coeur loyal!
Et sur mon corps sanglant, Marchez pour rendre hommage
A mon fils! Revêtu de mon manteau real!

THE PEOPLE *falling back in fear*   †

Hearing that voice!
At his words, God himself takes his part!
If we kill, God will curse us!

Ah! Cette voix!
Ces regards! Dieu lui-même a parlé!
Sur nos fronts va tomber l'anathème!

During this scene, a page has entered, slipping through the crowd. He approaches Don Carlos and throws a cape over his shoulders. The page is Eboli, who, before leaving, approaches the Queen.

EBOLI *aside, to the Queen*

You see how much I loved him!
I hastened through the streets and roused the people's anger,
And I have saved his life!
The cloister awaits me!
Farewell, my Queen!

Voyez si je l'aimais!
Courant les carrefours j'ai soulevé le peuple,
Et j'ai sauvé ses jours!
Le cloître m'attend!
Adieu, Reine!

ELISABETH

How can I bear this anguish?   Je me soutiens à peine.

PHILIP

Do not delay!   Frappez-moi, donc! †

THE INQUISITOR *appearing at the rear, surrounded by monks*

On your knees!   A genoux!

COUNT LERMA, COURTIERS, THE PEOPLE *drawing back*

The Grand Inquisitor!   Le Grand Inquisiteur!

THE INQUISITOR

You sacrilegious rabble,
Upon your knees, before the King, by God elected!
On your knees! On your knees!

O peuple sacrilège,
Prosterne-toi, devant celui que Dieu protège!
A genoux! A genoux!

Aprite quei cancelli!

Ciel!

Il popol è in furor!

Aprite! Io lo vo'!

Grandi di Spagna, salvate il Re!

Morte ai ribelli! Evviva il Re!

Ebben, perché tardar? A ferir v'affrettate!

Sgozzate un vecchio Re, gente dal cor
   leal!
E sulla spoglia e sangue,
Ergetevi e gettate su Carlo,

Mio figliuol, la porpora real!

Ah! Quella voce! Quello sguardo!
Dio stesso ha parlato!
Su di noi ricadrà l'anatema!

Vedete se l'amavo!
Correndo per le strade e il volgo
   sollevando,
La vita gl'ho salvato!
Il chiostro m'attende!
Addio, Regina!

Io mi sostengo appena.

Colpite orsù!

Vi prostrate!

Il grand'Inquisitor!

                  Popol ribelle ed empio,
T'umilia al Re, che Dio protegge!

Vi prostrate! Vi prostrate!

§ According to the Paris libretto, Eboli
enters, masked, at the head of the
People. She comes in front of Carlos,
whom the People then drag away.

† This passage was cut before the first
Paris première.

*Rita Gorr as Eboli, Covent Garden, 1961
(photo: Houston Rogers, Theatre Museum
Collection)*

PHILIP AND THE INQUISITOR

On your knees!   A genoux!

Great God, glory to Thee!   Grand Dieu, gloire à Toi!

COUNT LERMA, THE GRANDEES OF SPAIN *sword in hand*

Long live the King!   Vive le Roi!

THE PEOPLE *prostrating themselves*

O Lord, grant us your grace!   Seigneur! Pardonnez-nous!

Benjamin Luxon (Rodrigo) and Joseph Gabriels (Don Carlos), ENO, 1974; conductor, Charles Mackerras, producer, Colin Graham, set designer, Christopher Morley, costume designer, Ann Curtis (photo: John Garner)

A terra!

Gran Dio, sia gloria a te!

Evviva il Re!

Signor, di noi pietà!

Don Garrard (Grand Inquisitor) and Paul Plishka (Philip), Canadian Opera, 1977 (photo: Robert C. Ragsdale)

Act Five *

The Cloister at San Yuste. Night, moonlight.

Scena. [E]

Elisabeth enters slowly, lost in thought, approaches the tomb of Charles V and kneels.

ELISABETH

King who vowed to renounce all the world [22] Toi qui sus le néant des grandeurs de ce
and its splendour, monde,
King who found in the tomb God's calm, Toi qui goûtes enfin la paix douce et
peaceful and tender, profonde,
If there are tears in Heaven, tears from a Si l'on répand encore des larmes dans le
heart that's broken, ciel,
Ah, bear these tears, carry my tears of grief Porte en pleurant mes pleurs aux pieds de
on high to mighty God! l'Eternel!

Carlos will be here! . . . Yes, he must leave Carlos va venir! . . . Oui! Qu'il parte, qu'il
me, and forget me . . . oublie . . .
For to Posa I swore I would help him and J'ai promis à Posa de veiller sur sa vie,
save him.
His task he must pursue, fame and glory Qu'il suive son chemin glorieux et béni!
await him!
As for me, my task is over and my life's at Pour moi, ma tâche est faite, et mon jour
an end! est fini!

France, my noble land, beloved in my France, noble pays, si cher à mon jeune âge!
childhood!
Fontainebleau! My heart overflows when I Fontainebleau! Mon coeur est plein de
recall you . . . votre image . . .
It was there that God received our vows of C'est là que Dieu reçut notre éternel
lasting love; serment:
And that eternal vow could not last one Et son éternité n'a duré qu'un moment . . .
brief hour . . .

O fair gardens of Spain, so sombre in the Beaux jardins espagnols, à l'heure pâle et
twilight, sombre,
And if Carlos returns to wander through Si Carlos doit encor s'arrêter sous votre
your shadows, ombre,
May the leaves, and the streams, crystal Que vos fleurs, vos gazons, vos fontaines,
fountains and flowers, vos bois,
Sing together of love, that love that once Chantent mon souvenir avec toutes leurs
was ours! voix!

[22] ELISABETH

Tu che le vanità conoscesti del mondo

E godi nell'avel il riposo profondo,

S'ancor si piange in cielo, piangi sul mio
dolore,
E porta il pianto mio al trono del Signor.

Carlo qui verrà! . . . Sì! che parta e scordi
omai . . .
A Posa di vegliar sui giorni suoi giurai.

Ei segua il suo destin, la gloria il traccerà,

Per me, la mia giornata a sera è giunta già!

Francia, nobile suol, sì caro ai miei
verd'anni!
Fontainebleau! vêr voi schiude il pensier i
vanni.
Eterno giuro d'amor, là, Dio da me ascoltò,

E quest'eternità un giorno sol durò.

Tra voi, vaghi giardin di questa terra ibera,

Se Carlo ancor dovrà fermar i passi a sera

Che le zolle, i ruscelli, i fonti, i boschi, i
fior,
Con le lor armonie cantino il nostro amor.

*The 'Disposizione Scenica' for San Yuste:
Acts Two and Five: on the right is a chapel
(illuminated in Act Two). Through a gilded
grille, the tomb of Charles V is visible. To
the left, a door leads to the outside. At the
back is the door to the cloister. A garden
with tall cypresses. 1: the backcloth; 2: arch;
3: arch; X: gilded grilles.*

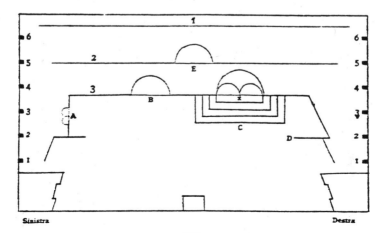

Farewell, dreams of delight . . . deceiving
    hopes! . . . delusions! . . .
I must break every bond which is tied to
    the world!
Farewell, my youth, my love! I succumb to
    my grief;
My heart knows one desire, for the peace of
    the tomb!

King who vowed to renounce all this world
    and its splendour,
King who found in the tomb God's calm,
    peaceful and tender,
If there are tears in Heaven, tears from a
    heart that's broken,
Ah, bear these tears, carry my tears of grief
    on high to mighty God!

O noble Emperor, you are now in
    Heaven,
Ah, if there are tears in Heaven, then bear
    my tears to God!

Duet.

DON CARLOS *appearing*

She's there!

ELISABETH

                A word . . . one word, the time
    has come to say farewell,
And we must part, and then your duty calls
    you;
You must live and forget me!

DON CARLOS

                Yes, now I will be strong;
But when my heart is breaking, I die before
    my death!

ELISABETH

No! Remember Rodrigo. Was it for foolish
    dreams
That he sacrificed his life?

DON CARLOS

In that fair land of Flanders he loved so well,
    I shall raise high his tomb,
More great that any king's, where his
    memory shall live.

ELISABETH

The sweetest flowers of Heaven will bloom
    on high to bring him joy and comfort!

DON CARLOS

I was lost in a dream! . . . it fled! . . . now,
    by the sombre light of day,
I see the flames destroying all the land,
The rivers red with blood, and a country
    laid waste,
A people in despair, who raise their hands
    to me,
Looking to me to help and save them from
    destruction.
And there I mean to go, to free them,
    though I live or die;

Adieu, rêve doré . . . illusion! . . .
    chimère! . . .
Tout lien est brisé qui m'attache à la terre!

Adieu, jeunesse, amour! . . . Succombant
    sous l'effort,
Mon coeur n'a qu'un seul voeu, c'est la
    paix dans la mort!

Toi qui sus le néant des grandeurs de ce
    monde,
Toi qui goûtes enfin la paix douce et
    profonde,
Si l'on répand encore des larmes dans le
    ciel,
Porte en pleurant mes pleurs aux pieds de
    l'Eternel!

Ame glorieuse envolée au ciel,

Ah, porte en pleurant mes pleurs aux pieds
    de l'Eternel!

                                    *

C'est elle!

                Un mot . . . un seul, le mot qui
    recommande
A Dieu celui qui part; après je vous demande

D'oublier et de vivre!

                Oui, je veux être fort;
Mais quand l'amour se brise, il tue avant la
    mort.

Non! Songez à Rodrigue. Est-ce pour des
    chimères
Qu'il s'est sacrifié?

                Dans ses Flandres si chères,
D'abord je veux lui faire élever un tombeau,
Comme jamais un roi n'en obtint de plus
    beau.

Les fleurs du Paradis réjouiront son
    ombre!

J'avais fait un beau rêve! . . . il fuit! . . . et le
    jour sombre
Me montre un incendie illuminant les airs,
Un fleuve teint de sang, des villages déserts,

Un peuple agonisant, et qui vers moi
    s'adresse
Comme à son Dieu sauveur, au jour de sa
    détresse.
A lui j'accours; heureux si, quel que soit
    mon sort,

Addio, bei sogni d'ôr . . . illusion
   perduta! . . .
Il nodo si spezzò, la luce è fatta muta!

Addio, verd'anni ancor! . . . cedendo al duol
   crudel,
Il cor ha un sol desir: la pace dell'avel!

Tu che le vanità conoscesti del mondo

E godi nell'avel il riposo profondo,

S'ancor si piange in cielo, piangi sul mio
   dolore,
E porta il pianto mio al trono del Signor.

Se ancor si piange in cielo,

Ah, il pianto mio reca a' pie' del Signor.

* From here to the end of the opera,
Verdi made several revisions and finally
recomposed it for Milan (see the
appendix for the text of this version).

E dessa!

   Un detto, un sol; al ciel io raccomando

Il pellegrin che parte; e poi sol vi domando

E l'oblio e la vita.

            Sì, forte esser vogl'io:
Ma quando è infranto amore, pria della
   morte uccide.

No, pensate a Rodrigo che per più grand'idee

Fin la sua vita diè.

            Là nel suolo fiammingo
Io vo'a lui fare un avel,
Come giammai Sovran ne vanto più bel!

I fiori schiusi in cielo a lui sorrideranno.

Sogno dorato io feci! . . . ei sparve! . . . or
   nell'affanno
Veggo un rogo feral spinger la fiamma al ciel.
Tinto di sangue un rio, i campi in duol
   crudel,
Un popol che si muor, e a me la man
   protende
Come al Dio salvator, nei dì della
   sventura.
A lui n'andrò beato, o spento o vincitor,

*Leona Mitchell as Elisabeth, Canadian
Opera, 1988 (photo: Robert C. Ragsdale)*

137

You'll rejoice in my victory or weep for my death!

Vous chantez mon triomphe ou pleurez sur ma mort!

ELISABETH

Ah, you speak as a hero and sacred flames inspire you,
And love worthy of us, yes, love that is pure and true,
Love that can change men to Gods! Ah! You must not delay.
Go, mount your cross and save those men who call for you!

Oui, voilà l'héroïsme avec ses nobles flammes,
L'amour digne de nous, l'amour des grandes âmes,
Qui font de l'homme un dieu! Va, sans perdre un instant,
Va, monte au Calvaire, et sauve un peuple qui t'attend!

DON CARLOS

Yes, in your voice I hear all the people of Flanders call,
Ah, if I die for them, then my blood is not shed in vain!
And only yesterday, no earthly power, I swear,
Could tear my hand from yours when once I held it fast,
But duty now has triumphed over tender weakness;
The star of glory shines to fill my heart with courage.
And see, Elisabeth! I can hold you in my arms,
Hold you and feel no faltering, yes, I am free at last!
Now that all's at an end, and my hand sadly
Draws away from yours . . . you are weeping?

Oui, c'est par votre voix que le peuple m'appelle,
Et si je meurs pour lui, que ma mort sera belle!
Hier, hier encor, aucun pouvoir humain
N'aurait pu séparer ma main de cette main,
Mais aujourd'hui l'honneur sur mon amour l'emporte;
Ma noble mission m'a fait une âme forte.
Voyez, Elisabeth! Je vous tiens dans mes bras,
Et ma vertu me reste et je ne fléchis pas!
Lorsque tout est fini, quand ma main se retire
De vos mains . . . vous pleurez?

ELISABETH

       Yes, yes, but I admire you;
These tears are tears of courage, tears that show noble grief,
Tears that all women shed when heroes must say farewell!

We shall meet not in this world, but where [23] life has no ending,
Far from this earthly strife where lasting peace enfolds us.

       Oui, mais je vous admire,
Ce sont les pleurs de l'âme, et de nobles sanglots,
Que les femmes toujours accordent aux héros!

[23] Au revoir dans un monde où la vie est meilleure,
Où l'avenir sans fin sonne la première heure;

[23] ACT FIVE - Duet

ELISABETH

Assai sostenuto

dans un mon - de | où la vi - - - e est meil -
ci ve - dre - mo | in un mon - - - do mi -
not in this world | but where life _____ has no

138

Se il plauso o il pianto avrò dal tuo cor!

Sì, l'eroismo è questo e il suo nobil ardore!

L'amor degno di noi, l'amor delle
    grand'alme,
Ei fa dell'uomo un Dio! Va, nel fiammingo
    suol!
Va, monta al Calvario e salva un popol
    nel duol!

Sì, per la voce tua il popol m'appella . . .

E se per lui morrò, la mia morte fia bella!

Ma pria di questo dì nessun poter uman

Disgiunta non avria la mia dalla tua man!

Quest'oggi l'onor potrà più dell'amore;

Sì nobil gesta diè più forte al cor vigore!

Or ben, Elisabetta! sul mio cor or sei tu,

Ma la virtù . . . l'onore mi rendon forte
    ancor!
Or se tutto finì se la mia man ritiro

Dalla tua man . . . tu piangi?

                     Sì, piango, ma t'ammiro.
Il pianto egli è dell'alma, e veder tu lo
    puoi,
Quel pianto san versar le donne per gli
    eroi!

Ma lassù ci vedremo in un mondo migliore,

Dell'avvenire eterno suonan per noi già
    l'ore;

Mirella Freni (Elisabeth) and Plácido Domingo (Don Carlos), Metropolitan Opera, 1983 (photo: Winnie Klotz)

Yes, there we'll meet again in the peace of the Lord,	Et là, nous trouverons dans la paix du Seigneur,
In that eternal calm which all men yearn to find!	Cet éternel absent qu'on nomme le bonheur!

ELISABETH AND DON CARLOS

We shall not meet in this world, but where life has no ending, *etc.*	Au revoir dans un monde où la vie est meilleure, *etc.*

ELISABETH

In this solemn hour of parting, we must use no words of weakness . . .	Au moment solonnel point d'indigne faiblesse . . .

ELISABETH AND DON CARLOS

We'll forget the vows of passion, vows that tell of earthly love!	Oublions tous les noms de profane tendresse!
We'll forget all the names that we murmured together.	Donnons-nous ces noms chers aux plus chastes amours.

DON CARLOS

Farewell, my mother!	Adieu, ma mère!

ELISABETH

Farewell, my son!	Adieu, mon fils!

ELISABETH AND DON CARLOS

Yes, we must part!	Et pour toujours!
Farewell!	Adieu!

Philip, the Grand Inquisitor and officials of the Inquisition enter.

Finale.

PHILIP *taking the Queen by the arm*

Yes, you must part! A two-fold sacrifice is needed!	Oui, pour toujours! Il faut un double sacrifice!
I've accomplished my task.	Je ferai mon devoir.

to the Inquisitor

And you?	Et vous?

THE INQUISITOR

The Holy Church Will do her part!	Le Saint-Office Fera le sien! . . .

PHILIP *indicating Don Carlos*

[I deliver to you this criminal, O sacred ministers of Heaven's vengeance!	Je vous livre ce criminel, O ministres sacrés des vengeances du ciel!
To you the unworthy son whom God allowed to be born of me!	A vous l'indigne fils que de moi Dieu fit naître! §
An abominable love blazes in him . . . To you, this traitor!]	Un détestable amour le brûle . . . à vous ce traître!

ELISABETH

[God will judge him!]	Dieu le jugera!

DON CARLOS

[God will judge me!]	Dieu me jugera!

CHOIR OF MONKS AND INQUISITION OFFICIALS

[God has declared it, Let the traitor be accursed!]	Dieu l'a dit, Que le traître soit maudit!

THE INQUISITOR

[To you this despiser of the Catholic faith, This friend of Posa, this forsworn heretic!]	A vous ce contempteur de la foi catholique, Cet ami de Posa, ce parjure hérétique!

E là noi troverem nel pace del ciel

Quel bene che perdè quest'alma mia
    fedel!

Ma lassù ci vedremo in un mondo migliore,
etc.

Nell'ora dell'addio sia forte il nostro petto,

Tutti i nomi scordiam d'ogni profàno
    affetto.
Profferiamo gli accenti cari a' più casti
    amor.

Addio, mia madre!

      Mio figlio, addio!

                    Eterno addio!
Per sempre, addio!

*Carlo Cossutta (Don Carlos) and Katia
Ricciarelli (Elisabeth), Bayerische
Staatsoper, Munich, 1975 (photo: Anne
Kirchbach)*

Sì, eterno addio! Io voglio un doppio
    sacrifizio!
Il mio dover farò.

      E voi?

                   Il Santo Uffizio
Il suo farà!

Lascio al vostro rigor il reo,
O ministri del ciel d'un Dio vendicator!
Il figlio indegno è questo che a me diede
    il Signore.
Reo d'un iniquo amor . . . vi cedo il traditore!

§ A vous ce fils ingrat que de moi Dieu
fit naître!

Fia giudice il ciel!

Fia giudice il ciel!

          Dio lo vuol!
Maledetto il traditor!

A voi chi calpestò la cattolica fede,
Di Posa amico fu, eresiarca indegno!

141

CHORUS

[God has declared it,
Let the heretic be accurst!]

Dieu l'a dit,
L'hérétique soit maudit!

PHILIP

[To you this seducer of my faithful subjects,
This enemy of kings and of God . . .
this rebel!]

A vous ce séducteur de mon peuple fidèle,
Cet ennemi des rois et de Dieu,
ce rebelle!

PHILIP, THE INQUISITOR, CHORUS

[Be accurst! Author of a deed detested!
Be accurst, and your ashes scattered
to the whirlwind!
Banished from the celestial realm of
shining peace,
Heretic, rebel and traitor, be accurst!]

Sois maudit, artisan d'une oeuvre détestée!
Sois maudit, et ta cendre à l'ouragan
jetée!
Chassé du lieu céleste où la paix
resplendit,
Hérétique, rebelle et traître, sois maudit!

ELISABETH

[Of our chaste farewells these executioners
make crimes.
They require two victims.
Horror! God will judge!]

§
De nos chastes adieux ces bourreaux font
des crimes,
Il leur faut deux victimes.
Horreur! Dieu jugera!

DON CARLOS

[Purveyors of death,
They require two victims.
Lies! God will judge!]

Pourvoyeurs de la mort,
Il leur faut deux victimes.
Mensonge! Dieu jugera!

THE INQUISITOR *to the officials of the Inquisition, indicating Don Carlos*

[Guards!]

Gardes!

PHILIP

[My son is no more!]

Mon fils n'est plus!

DON CARLOS *in despair*

[Ah, God will avenge me!
This bloody tribunal, His hand will shatter it!]

Ah! Dieu me vengera!
Ce tribunal de sang, sa main le brisera!

Don Carlos, defending himself, retreats towards the tomb of Charles V. The grille opens. The Monk
appears, takes Don Carlos in his arms and covers him with his mantle.

CHARLES V (THE MONK)

My son, though the griefs that assailed you
Must still be endured in this place,
The peace that your heart so yearns for
Will be found at the throne of grace!

Mon fils, les douleurs de la terre
Nous suivent encor dans ce lieu. §§
La paix que votre coeur espère
Ne se trouve qu'auprès de Dieu!

THE INQUISITOR

That's the Emperor's voice!

La voix de l'Empereur!

CHOIR OF MONKS

The Emperor Charles!

C'est Charles-Quint!

PHILIP *in terror*

My father!

Mon père!

ELISABETH

Oh God!

Grand Dieu!

The Monk leads the dazed Don Carlos into the cloister. ◊
The curtain falls slowly.

CHOIR OF MONKS *offstage*

Charles V, our mighty Lord,
Lies here in dust and lifeless clay!

[6] Charles-Quint, l'auguste Empereur,
N'est plus que cendre et que poussière. §§§

The end of the opera.

142

L'eresiarca cada al suol!

Dio lo vuol!

E questo il seduttor del popol mio fedele,
A Dio nemico al Re, morrà questo
ribelle!

Maledetto! Compisti un'opra abbominata!
Tu morrai e la polve al vento fia gettata!

Maledetto dal cielo, maledetto quaggiù!

Eresiarca, ribelle, traditore, tu morrai!

Dell'amor nostro casto costor fanno
un delitto,
Di due vittime han d'uopo.
Orror! Dio giudicherà!

§ The verses for Elisabeth and Carlos
do not appear in the libretto.

Una alor non bastò,
Di due vittime han d'uopo.
Menzogna! Dio giudicherà!

Guardie!

L'Infante muor!

Ah! Vindice fia Dio!
Un tribunal di sangue sua mano struggerà!

Il duolo della terra
Nel chiostro ancor ci segue.
Solo del cor la guerra
In ciel si calmerà!

§§ Viennent expirer en ce lieu,

Oh ciel! L'Imperator!

E Carlo Quinto!

Mio padre!

Oh ciel!

◊ According to the *Disposizione Scenica*,
Elisabeth gives thanks to Heaven, while
Charles V drags Don Carlos into the
cloister.

§§§
CHOIR OF MONKS *in the chapel*
Au jour terrible où le pécheur
N'est plus que cendre et que poussière,
Que les traits de votre colère
Se détournent de lui, Seigneur!

Carlo il sommo Imperatore,
Polve e cenere sol è.

143

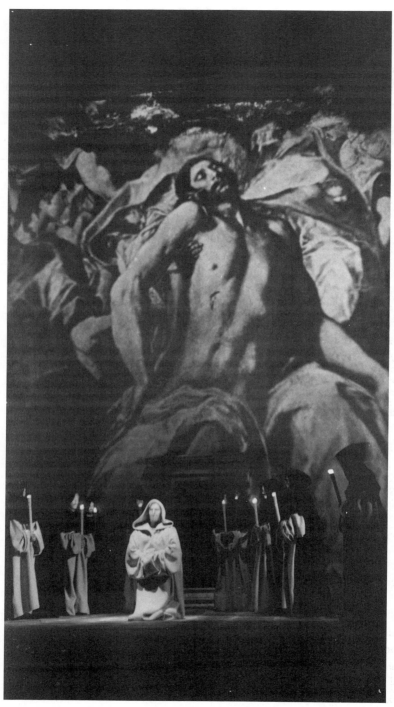

Ingmar Korjus as the Monk, Canadian Opera, 1977 (photo: Robert C. Ragsdale)

Appendix

These are extracts from the libretto devised for the four-act version in Italian given at La Scala, Milan, in 1884. Only scenes which involve major alterations to the text are included here. They were written for Verdi in French by Camille du Locle, translated by Angelo Zanardini, and form part of the translation attributed to de Lauzières and Zanardini.

Act One, Scene One
corresponding to Act Two, scene one of the 1867 version: see page 53

The cloister of the monastery of San Yuste. [After the opening 'Scene and Prayer' [5], retitled by Verdi 'Prelude', Carlos appears wandering in the cloister. As the monks leave, he steps forward.]

Allegro agitato

DON CARLOS

And I have lost her! O ye powers above!
Another, and he my father . . . another,
and he the King . . .
He has seized her whom I love so!
My bride, my fair betrothed . . . Ah, I recall
that calm, fair
Day, which had no morrow, when, our
hearts filled with hope,
She and I were quite alone, alone in the
silence
Of France so fair and lovely,
In the woods of Fontainebleau!

There I saw her, there I was captured,
With her smile she stole my heart!
There I swore we would live united,
There I told her we would never part.
But that spring had no summer days to
follow,
Stars conspired against us above,
And I lost in a single moment
My heart, my life, and all my love!

Io l'ho perduta! Oh, potenza suprema!
Un altro . . . ed è mio padre! un altro . . . e
quest'è il Re.
Lei che adoro m'ha rapita!
La sposa a me promessa! Ah! Quanto puro
e bello fu il dì,
Il dì senza diman, in cui ebri di speme,

C'era dato vagar nell'ombra, soli insieme,

Nel dolce suol di Francia,
Nella foresta di Fontainebleau!

Io la vidi e il suo sorriso
Nuovo un ciel apriva a me!
Ah! Per sempre or m'ha diviso
Da quel core un padre, un re.
Non prometti un dì felice

Di mia vita il triste albor,
M'hai rubato, incantatrice,
E cor, e speme, e sogni, e amor!

The Monk has stopped to listen to Carlos, and addresses him before he disappears into the cloister. Don Carlos exclaims 'La sua voce! [. . .] O terror! O terror!' Rodrigo enters.

Allegro agitato

RODRIGO

There he is! There's the Prince!

E lui! Desso! L'infante!

DON CARLOS

      O my Rodrigo!

      O mio Rodrigo!

RODRIGO

      Your Highness!

      Altezza!

DON CARLOS

My friend! How gladly I embrace you!

Sei tu ch'io stringo al seno!

RODRIGO

Dearest Carlos! My friend!

O mio prence . . . signor!

DON CARLOS

A friend, whom God has sent to ease my
grief,
Angel of strength and hope!

E il ciel che a me t'invia nel mio dolor,

Angel consolator!

RODRIGO

My dearest comrade!
The hour has struck! In Flanders they call
  for a saviour!
They must not call in vain, and you alone
  can help!
But what is this? Why do you grow so
  pale?
Why this flash of despair that I see in
  your glances?
And not a word! ... You only sigh! ...
  You weep!
Dearest Carlos, let me share
Your grief and calm your pain!

DON CARLOS

Ah, my comrade, my friend, my brother,
Let me mourn, let me weep in your
  arms!

RODRIGO

Hear the voice of the friend who loves you.
Open your heart, let me share your grief!
Tell me!

DON CARLOS

Shall I tell? Then learn all my sorrow!
Yes, learn what fearful blow
Fate has struck in my heart!
I love, with a passionate fire, Elisabeth!

RODRIGO *horrified*

Your mother! God in Heaven!

DON CARLOS

                    Yes, I know ...
You're unable to look in my eyes ... then
  I'm lost!
My Rodrigo forsakes me. Rodrigo turns
  away
And renounces his friend!

RODRIGO

                    Your Rodrigo loves you!
And I swear by my faith,
You suffer ... that is all in the world that
  I see!

DON CARLOS

O my Rodrigo!

RODRIGO

My Carlos! As the King has not yet
  discovered your secret ...

DON CARLOS

No!

RODRIGO

You must ask his leave to depart now for
  Flanders.
Thus by a deed worthy of you,
Conquer your heart ... and you shall learn
  there,

O amato prence!
L'ora suonò! Te chiama il popolo
fiammingo!
Soccorrer tu lo dêi; ti fa suo salvator!

Ma che ved'io! Quale pallor, qual pena!

Un lampo di dolor sul ciglio tuo balena,

Muto sei tu! ... Sospiri! ... Hai triste il
cor!
Carlo mio, con me, dividi
Il tuo pianto, il tuo dolor.

Mio salvator, mio fratel, mio fedele,
Lascia ch'io pianga in seno a te!

Versami in cor il tuo strazio crudele,
L'anima tua non sia chiusa per me!
Parla!

Lo vuoi tu? La mia sventura apprendi,
E qual orrendo stral
Il mio cor trapassò!
Amo ... d'un colpevole amor ...
    Elisabetta!

Tua madre! Giusto ciel!

                    Qual pallor!
Lo sguardo chini al suol ... Tristo me!

Tu stesso, mio Rodrigo,

T'allontani da me!

                    No, Rodrigo ancor t'ama!
Io tel posso giurar.
Tu soffri! Già per me l'universo dispar!

O mio Rodrigo!

Mio prence! Questo arcano dal Re non fu
sorpreso ancora?

No!

Ottien dunque da lui di partir per la
Fiandra.
Taccia il tuo cor, degna di te
Opra farai; apprendi omai

Among those suffering people how a king should rule!	In mezzo a gente oppressa a divenir un Re!

DON CARLOS

That brave advice I'll follow!	Ti seguirò, fratello.

A bell tolls.

RODRIGO

But listen! The cloister doors will soon be unbarred, admitting Your father and also the Queen.	Ascolta! Le porte de l'asil s'apron già; qui verranno Filippo e la Regina!

DON CARLOS

Elisabeth!	Elisabetta!

RODRIGO

O Carlos, at my side show resolve and rouse your fainting spirits! For there in Flanders the people wait to greet their saviour. We'll pray to God to fire your soul with strength!	Rinfranca accanto a me lo spirto che vacilla, Serena ancora la stella tua nei cieli brilla! Domanda al ciel dei forti la virtù!

[The duet and the rest of the scene follows as in the 1867 original.]

Act One, Scene Two
corresponding to Act Two, scene two of the 1867 version: see page 77

A delightful place at the gates of the monastery of San Yuste.

[This duet begins at the word 'Restate!', when Philip commands Rodrigo not to withdraw. The 1867 text was kept in the 1884 version until Philip's line 'Inerte può restar?']

RODRIGO

If Spain has need of a sword to defend her, If my country is wronged, if a foe should be near, Then my hand and my sword will be the first to serve her.	Ove alla Spagna una spada bisogni, Una vindice man, un custode all'onor, Bentosto brillerà la mia di sangue intrisa!

PHILIP

That I know . . . but, for now, what would you ask me?	Ben lo so . . . ma per voi che far poss'io?

RODRIGO

I! Nothing! Not for me! But, for others . . .	Nulla! No . . . nulla per me! Ma per altri . . .

PHILIP

What does that mean? Others?	Che vuoi dire? Per altri?

RODRIGO

Sire, I shall speak freely, If you will allow.	Io parlerò, Sire! Se grave non v'è!

PHILIP

Speak on!	Favella!

RODRIGO

O King, I come here from Flanders,
From that country once so fair!
That is now but a desert of ashes,
A place of death and despair!
There in the streets there are orphans,
They're starving and beg for food,
Stumbling as they flee from the fire clouds,
Smeared with their own parents' blood!
The streams are laden with corpses,
The rivers with blood run red,
And the air is loud with shrieking
Of women who mourn for their dead.
Ah! Dear God be praised for this meeting!
Thy hand has led me to bring
The news of Flanders in torment
Before my King!

O Signor, di Fiandra arrivo,
Quel paese un dì si bel!
D'ogni luce or fatto privo
Ispira orror, par muto avel!
L'orfanel che non ha loco
Per le vie piangendo va;
Tutto struggon ferro e foco,
Bandita è la pietà!
La riviera che rosseggia
Scorrer sangue al guardo par;
Della madre il grido echeggia
Pei figlioli che spirar!
Ah! Sia benedetto Iddio,
Che narrar lascia a me
Questa cruda agonia
Perché sia nota al Re.

PHILIP

Blood is the price that's paid for peace [D]
in my dominions.
My thunderbolt has crushed those proud
rebellious men,
Who sought to plunge our people in
false, lying dreams!
And death, sown by my own hands, has
brought its harvest.

Col sangue sol potei la pace aver del
mondo;
Il brando mio calcò l'orgoglio ai novator

Che illudono le genti coi sogni mentitor!

La morte in questa man ha un avvenir
fecondo.

RODRIGO

So! Do you believe that, sowing death,
You sow for future peace?

Che! Voi pensate, seminando morte,
Piantar per gli anni eterni?

PHILIP

Look at Spain, there's your answer!
Where the workmen in the towns, the
peasants in the country,
Accept the laws of God and the rule of
their King!
I'll bring that kind of peace to my Flanders!

Volgi un guardo alle Spagne!
L'artigian cittadin, la plebe alle campagne

A Dio fedel e al Re un lamento non ha!

La pace stessa io dono alle mie Fiandre!

RODRIGO

A mockery of peace! The peace that fills
the grave!
O King! Would you have future ages
Curse your name and say: 'A second
Nero!'
What kind of peace is this you give your
subjects?
What do you bring them but fear and
horrors unending?
Your priests are men of blood and your
soldiers beasts of prey!
Your people die and their groans have
been silenced.
And all your empire is a wasted desert,

Where the name of King Philip is accurst!
You could spread, great as God, joy and
peace through your empire.
King, rouse yourself, show yourself
sublime!
A word from you could change your life,
and set your people free!

Orrenda, orrenda pace! La pace è dei
sepolcri!
O Re, non abbia mai
Di voi l'istoria a dir: Ei fu Neron!

Quest'è la pace che voi date al mondo?

Desta tal don terror, orror profondo!

E un carnefice il prete, un bandito ogni
armier!
Il popol geme e si spegne tacendo,

E il vostro imper deserto immenso,
orrendo,
S'ode ognun a Filippo maledir!
Come un Dio redentor, l'orbe inter
rinnovate,
V'ergete a vol sublime, sovra d'ogn'altro
Re!
Per voi, si allieti il mondo! Date la
libertà!

PHILIP

Strange and fantastic dreams!
You'd quickly change your mind if you
   but knew
The hearts of men as they're known by
   their ruler!
Say no more . . . The King has not heard
   what you said . . .
Have no fear!
But you beware my Grand Inquisitor! . . .

Oh! Strano sognator!
Tu muterai pensier, se il cor dell'uom

Conoscerai qual Filippo il conosce!

Or non più! Ha nulla inteso il Re!

Non temer!
Ma ti guarda dal Grande Inquisitor!

RODRIGO

What! . . . Sire! . . .

Che! Sire!

PHILIP

You have stood here in my presence,
And asked no favour for yourself from
   the King.
I appoint you to my personal service.

Tu resti in mia regal presenza
E nulla ancor hai domando al Re?

Io voglio averti a me d'accanto!

RODRIGO

               Sire!
No! Let me stay as I am!

               Sire!
No! Quel ch'io son restar io vo'.

PHILIP

        You are too proud!
You dared to lift your eyes and gaze on [13]
   me as a ruler,
But did you see the heavy load of sorrow
That weighs on the man beneath the crown?
Can you guess at my grief, the troubles
   that surround me?
Made wretched by my son, tortured by
   my own wife!

            Sei troppo alter!
Osò lo sguardo tuo penetrar il mio soglio.

Dal capo mio che grava la corona,
L'angoscia apprendi e il duol!
Guarda or tu la mia reggia! L'affano la
   circonda . . .
Sgraziato genitor! Sposo più triste ancor!

RODRIGO

Sire, what can you mean?

Sire, che dite mai!

PHILIP

The Queen . . . I am racked by suspicion!
My son! . . .

La Regina . . . Un sospetto mi turba . . .
Mio figlio!

RODRIGO *impetuously*

    His heart is pure and noble . . .

    Fiera ha l'alma insieme pura!

PHILIP *with an outburst of grief*

All I love in the world is stolen by my
   son!

Nulla val sotto al ciel il ben che tolse a
   me!

Rodrigo looks at Philip appalled, and makes no reply.

Be you their judge and my support!
And sound those hearts which love
   draws on to madness!
By my leave you may speak when you
   wish to the Queen . . .
You alone in my Court, you alone are a
   man.
I take my heart and place it in your
   hands!

Il lor destin affido a te!
Scruta quei cor, che un folle amor
   trascina!
Sempre lecito è a te di scontrar la
   Regina!
Tu, che sol sei un uom, fra lo stuolo
   uman!
Ripongo il cor nella leal tua man.

RODRIGO

(A sudden ray of hope inspires me!
The King has bared that heart which
   was always closed before!)

(Inaspettata aurora in ciel appar!
S'aprì quel cor che niun potè scrutar!)

PHILIP

Ah! May this day of hope restore my peace of mind!

Possa cotanto dì la pace a me tornar!

RODRIGO

(A sudden ray of hope inspires me!)

(Oh, sogno mio divin! O gloriosa speme!)

PHILIP

But beware my Grand Inquisitor!
Oh, beware! Yes, beware!

Ti guarda dal Grande Inquisitor!
Ti guarda! Ti guarda!

RODRIGO

Sire!

Sire!

The King extends his hand to Rodrigo, who kneels before him and kisses it.

The curtain falls quickly.

End of Act One.

Act Three, Scene One
corresponding to Act Four, scene one of the 1867 version: see page 113

The King's Study in Madrid.

Scena and Quartet.

[This scene begins with the 'Allegro agitato' when Elisabeth rushes into Philip's study: 'Giustizia! Sire.' The 1884 text follows the 1867 original until this point, and the text for 'O don fatale' at the end remains the same.]

PHILIP

Here's a portrait of Carlos!
Have you nothing to tell me?
Here's a portrait of Carlos!

Il ritratto di Carlo!
Non trovate parola?
Il ritratto di Carlo!

ELISABETH

      Yes!

      Sì.

PHILIP

      Concealed with your jewels?

      Fra i vostri gioiel?

ELISABETH

Yes!

Sì.

PHILIP

      What! You dare confess that to me?

      Che! Confessar l'osate a me!

ELISABETH

      Yes, I dare!
You know full well I was betrothed,
To Don Carlos, yes, to your son!
I came to you, at God's command,
Pure as the fleur-de-lys of France!
Yet you dare, driven mad by suspicion,
Cast doubt on a daughter of France,
Cast doubt on the word of a princess,
Doubt the Queen . . . doubt me!

      Io l'oso! Sì!
Ben lo sapete, un dì promessa
A figlio vostro fu la mia man!
Or v'appartengo, a Dio sommessa.
Ma immacolata qual giglio son.
Ed ora si sospetta
L'onor d'Elisabetta! . . .
Si dubita di me . . .
E chi m'oltraggia è il Re!

PHILIP

You're far too bold, you speak too freely!
So far you've only known me in my moments of weakness.
That weakness will not last; you'll see it turn to rage.
And then, beware! Beware!

Ardita troppo voi favellate!
Me debole credete e sfidarmi sembrate;

La debolezza in me può diventar furor.

Tremate allor per voi, per me.

150

ELISABETH

And what has been my crime?

Il mio fallir qual è?

PHILIP

You lied to me!
If your disgrace is as deep as I think it,
If you've betrayed me . . . then by God high
 above,
I swear to be revenged with blood!

Spergiura!
Se tanta infamia colmò la misura,
Se fui da voi tradito, io lo giuro innanzi al
 ciel.
Il sangue verserò!

ELISABETH

How I pity you!

Pietà mi fate.

PHILIP

You dare pity me? An adulterous wife!

Ah! la pietà d'adultera consorte!

ELISABETH *swooning*

Ah!

Ah!

PHILIP *opening the doors*

Come and help the Queen!

Soccorso alla Regina!

Eboli enters hastily, Rodrigo a little later.

EBOLI *alarmed as she sees the Queen in a swoon*

(Ah! What have I done? Alas!)

(Ciel! che mai feci! . . . Ahimè!)

RODRIGO *to Philip*

Sire! . . . When half of this world looks to
 you as its ruler,
One man alone you have failed to
 subdue!
The King has no power to command
 himself?

Sire! . . . soggetta è a voi la metà della
 terra;
Sareste dunque in tanto vasto imper

Il sol, cui non v'è dato il comandar?

PHILIP

(Accurst be this hour, o unworthy
 suspicion,
Work of a cruel fiend sent from Hell!
No! She is proud and she is honest,
I know her soul is pure and true!)

(Ah! sii maledetto, sospetto fatale,

Opera d'un demon infernal!
[19] No, non macchiò la fè giurata,
A me infedel costei non fu!)

EBOLI

(O remorse! O regret unavailing!
I have sinned, committed a crime, o
 remorse!
Ah! I've betrayed my innocent Queen!
How can I hope now for peace?)

(La perdei! o rimorso fatale!
Commettea un delitto infernal!

Io tradia quel nobile cor!
Io ne morrò dal dolor!

RODRIGO

(The time has come, I hear the thunder,
The lightning flashes and I must act.
This land of Spain requires a victim,
Who will die to ensure future peace!)

(Omai d'oprar suonata è l'ora,
Folgor orrenda in ciel brillò!
Che per la Spagna un uomo mora . . .
Lieto avvenir le lascerò.)

ELISABETH *coming to*

Where am I? Alas! Ah, see me, mother!
See these tears that burn in my eyes.
Alone in this country so unfriendly!
Grant, oh God, grant me peace!

Che avvenne! O ciel! In pianto e duolo
Ognun, o madre, m'abbandonò,
Io son straniera in questo suol,
Più sulla terra speme non ho!

The King, after a moment of hesitation, leaves. Rodrigo makes a decisive gesture and follows him.
Eboli remains alone with the Queen.

Scena and Aria

EBOLI *throwing herself at Elisabeth's feet*

Forgive and pardon a woman who's
  wronged you!

Pietà! perdon! per la rea che si pente.

ELISABETH

Why do you kneel? What is it?

Al mio pie'! Voi! Qual colpa?

EBOLI

  Ah! My remorse overwhelmes me!
My heart will break with grief!
Angel from Heaven, o my Queen true and
  noble,
Now learn what cruel fiend from Hell has
  worked your ruin!
Your case of jewels was stolen by me!

  Ah! m'uccide il rimorso!
Torturato è il mio cor.
Angel del ciel, Regina augusta e pia,

Sappeate a qual demon l'inferno vi dà in
  preda!
Quello scrigno ... son io che l'involai.

ELISABETH

You!

Voi!

EBOLI

  Yes, I it was accused you!

Si, son io, son io che v'accusai!

ELISABETH

What, you!

Voi!

EBOLI

Yes, my love and my rage,
The hate I felt for you!
Passion and fury combined to torment me
And jealousy poisoned my heart!
I loved Don Carlos! By him I was rejected!

Sì ... l'amor, il furor,
L'odio che avea per voi ...
La gelosia crudel che straziavami il cor
Contro voi m'eccitar.
Io Carlo amava, e Carlo m'ha sprezzata!

ELISABETH

You loved the Prince! Rise again!

Voi l'amaste? Sorgete.

EBOLI

  No! No! Forgive! Forgive!
There's more to tell you!

  No! Pietà di me!
Un'altra colpa!

ELISABETH

  What more?

    Ancor!

EBOLI

  Forgive! Forgive! The King ...
Ah, do not curse me now ...
He ... the King, seduced me!
I who dared to accuse you, I myself was
  guilty!

  Pietà! Pietà! Il Re ...
Non imprecate a me!
Sì ... sedotta ... perduta ...
L'error che v'imputai ... io ... stessa ...
  avea commesso.

ELISABETH

Ah!

Ah!

She covers her face with her hands and turns away.

Return me your cross! Before tomorrow's
  dawn,
Be gone from my Court!
Between exile and the veil,
You now may choose!

Rendetemi la croce! ...

La Corte vi convien lasciar col dì novello!
Tra l'esilio ed il vel
Sceglier potrete!

She leaves.

Eboli *stands up again with the despairing cry 'Ah!' più non vedrò la Regina!'. The scene continues
with her aria 'O don fatale'. See page 121.*

152

Act Three, Scene Two
corresponding to Act Four, scene two in the 1867 version: see page 127

Don Carlos' prison.

[Variously called 'Emeute', 'Sommossa' or 'Insurrection'. Philip enters with the Grandees of Spain and Lerma after Rodrigo has died, and Carlos has thrown himself upon the corpse.]

PHILIP

My son, I return you your sword.

Mio Carlo, a te la spada io rendo!

DON CARLOS *in despair*

Stand back! For that hand is stained with
his blood!
Stand back! We'd sworn to live united
As brothers and he loved me! He gave his
life for me,
His only friend!

Arretra!

La tua man di sangue è intrisa! Orror!
Una fraterna fede ci univa . . . ei m'amava!

La vita sua per me sacrificò!

PHILIP

My fears were all too true!

Presagio mio feral!

DON CARLOS

No, you have no son from today.
All my kingdom is there with him!

Tu più figlio non hai! I regni miei
Stan presso a lui!

He throws himself again on Rodrigo's body.

PHILIP

Who will give me back that man?

Chi rende a me quell'uom?

The alarm bell sounds in the distance.

THE GRANDEES OF SPAIN

Ha! The alarm!

Ciel! suona a stormo!

COUNT LERMA

The mob is in revolt!
And they call for the Prince!

Il popol è in furor!
E l'Infante ch'ei vuol!

PHILIP

Unbar that doorway!

Si schiudan le porte!

COUNT LERMA, THE GRANDEES OF SPAIN

Sire!

Ciel!

PHILIP

Come, obey! Do my will!

Obbedite! Io lo vo'!

THE PEOPLE *in the distance*

He dies who dares oppose the might of the
people!
We strike to kill and have no fear!
The King himself must beware our fury,
Bow his head and do as we say!

Perir dovrà chi d'arrestarci attenti!

Feriam, feriam senza tema, o pietà!
Tremar dovrà e curvar la testa
Davanti al popol, al popol ultor!

The People enter in a fury.

EBOLI *masked, to Don Carlos*

Escape! Escape!

Va! fuggi!

PHILIP *to the People*

And whom do you seek?

Che volete?

153

THE PEOPLE

Don Carlos! — L'Infante!

PHILIP

There he stands. — Egli qui sta!

THE INQUISITOR

Sacrilegious rabble! — Sacrilegio infame!

THE PEOPLE *drawing back*

The Grand Inquisitor! ... — Il Grand'Inquisitor!

THE INQUISITOR

On your knees / Before the King, by God elected! / On your knees! On your knees! — Vi prostrate / Innanzi al Re, che Dio protegge! / Vi prostrate! Vi prostrate!

PHILIP AND THE INQUISITOR

On your knees! — A terra!

THE PEOPLE *prostrating themselves*

O Lord, grant us your grace! — Signor, di noi pietà!

PHILIP AND THE INQUISITOR

Great God, glory to Thee! — Gran Dio, sia gloria a Te!

COUNT LERMA, THE GRANDEES OF SPAIN *sword in hand*

Long live the King! — Evviva il Re!

The curtain falls.

End of Act Three.

Act Four

corresponding to Act Five in the 1867 version: see page 137

The cloister of the monastery of San Yuste: Scene and Farewell Duet and Final Scene.

[This scene begins with the entry of Don Carlos, 'E dessa!', but the words are the same in the 1867 version until this point.]

ELISABETH

No! Remember Rodrigo. Was it for foolish dreams / That he sacrificed his life? — No, pensate a Rodrigo! Non è per folli idee, / Ch'ei si sacrificò!

DON CARLOS

In that fair land of Flanders he loved so well, / I shall raise high his tomb, / More great that any king's, where his memory shall live. — Sulla terra fiamminga / Io vo' che a lui s'innalzi sublime, eccelso avel, / Qual mai ne ottenne un re tanto nobil e bel!

ELISABETH

The sweetest flowers of Heaven will bloom on high to bring him joy and comfort! — I fior del paradiso a lui sorrideranno.

DON CARLOS

I was lost in a dream! ... it fled! ... now, by the sombre light of day, / I see the flames destroying all the land, — Vago sogno m'arrise ... ei sparve! ... e nell'affanno / Un rogo appar a me, che spinge vampe al ciel.

The rivers red with blood, and a country laid waste, / A people in despair, who raise their hands to me, — Di sangue tinto un rio, resi i campi un avel, / Un popolo che muor, e a me la man protende,

154

Looking to me to help and save them from destruction.
And there I mean to go, to free them, though I live or die;
You'll rejoice in my victory or weep for my death!

ELISABETH

Ah, you speak as a hero and sacred flames inspire you,
And love worthy of us, yes, love that is pure and true,
Love that can change men to gods! Ah! You must not delay.
Go, mount your cross and save those men who call for you!

DON CARLOS

Yes, in your voice I hear all the people of Flanders call,
Ah, if I die for them, then my blood is not shed in vain!

And only yesterday, no earthly power, I swear,
Could tear my hand from yours when once I held it fast,
But duty now has triumphed over tender weakness;
The star of glory shines to fill my heart with courage.
And see, Elisabeth! I can hold you in my arms,
Hold you and feel no faltering, yes, I am free at last!
Now that all's at an end, and my hand sadly
Draws away from yours . . . you are weeping?

ELISABETH

Yes, yes, but I admire you;
These tears are tears of courage, tears that show noble grief,
Tears that all women shed when heroes must say farewell!

We shall meet not in this world, but where life has no ending,
Far from this earthly strife where lasting peace enfolds us.
Yes, there we'll meet again in the peace of the Lord,
In that eternal calm which all men yearn to find!

ELISABETH AND DON CARLOS

We shall not meet in this world, but where life has no ending, *etc.*

ELISABETH

In this solemn hour of parting, we must use no words of weakness . . .

Siccome a Redentor, nei dì della sventura.

A Lui n'andrò beato, se spento o vincitor,

Plauso o pianto m'avrò dal tuo memore cor.

Sì, l'eroismo è questo e la sua sacra fiamma!
L'amor degno di noi, l'amor che i forti infiamma!
Ei fa dell'uomo un Dio! Va! Di più non tardar!
Sali il Calvario e salva un popolo che muor!

Sì, con la voce tua quella gente m'appella . . .
E se morrò per lei, la mia morte fia bella!

Ma pria di questo dì alcun poter uman

Disgiunta non avria la mia dalla tua man!

Ma vinto in sì gran dì l'onor ha in me l'amore;
Impresa a questa par rinnova e mente e core!

Non vedi, Elisabetta, io ti stringo al mio sen,
Né mia virtù vacilla, né ad essa mancherò!

Or che tutto finì e la man io ritiro

Dalla tua man . . . tu piangi?

Sì, piango, ma t'ammiro!
Il pianto gli è dell'alma, e veder tu lo puoi,
Qual san pianto versar le donne per gli eroi!

Ma lassù ci vedremo in un mondo migliore,

Dell'avvenir eterno suonan per noi già l'ore;
E là noi troverem nel grembo del Signor,
Il sospirato ben che fugge in terra ognor!

Ma lassù ci vedremo in un mondo migliore, *etc.*

In tal dì, che per noi non avrà più domani.

ELISABETH AND DON CARLOS

We'll forget all the names that we
murmured together.

Tutti i nomi scordiam degli affetti profani.

DON CARLOS

Farewell, my mother!

Addio, mia madre!

ELISABETH

Farewell, my son!

Mio figlio, addio!

ELISABETH AND DON CARLOS

Yes, we must part!   Eterno addio!
Farewell!   Per sempre, addio!

Philip, the Grand Inquisitor and officials of the Inquisition enter.

PHILIP *taking the Queen by the arm*

Yes, you must part! A two-fold sacrifice is
needed!
I've accomplished my task.

Sì, per sempre! Io voglio un doppio
sacrifizio!
Il dover mio farò.

to the Inquisitor

And you?   Ma voi?

THE INQUISITOR

The Holy Church   Il Santo Uffizio
Will do her part!   Il suo farà!

ELISABETH

God!   Ciel!

THE INQUISITOR *to the officials of the Inquisition, indicating Don Carlos*

Seize him!   Guardie!

DON CARLOS

God will revenge my life!   Dio mi vendicherà!
Hands that are stained with blood shall   Il tribunal di sangue sua mano spezzerà!
never make me yield!

*Don Carlos, defending himself, retreats towards the tomb of Charles V. The grille opens; the Monk
appears. It is Charles V with mantle and royal crown.*

THE MONK

My son, though the griefs that assail you
Still must be endured in this place,
The peace that your heart so yearns for
Will be found at the throne of grace.

Il duolo della terra
Nel chiostro ancor ci segue;
Solo del cor la guerra
In ciel si calmerà.

THE INQUISITOR

That's the Emperor's voice!

E la voce di Carlo!

FOUR INQUISITION OFFICIALS

It's Charles the Fifth!   E Carlo Quinto!

PHILIP *startled and shocked*

My father!   Mio padre!

ELISABETH

Oh God!   Oh ciel!

The monk leads the dazed Don Carlos into the cloister.
The end of the opera.

Selective Discography

David Nice

Five-act version of 1886 with appendix of music from 1866-67, in French
Domingo (*Carlos*), Ricciarelli (*Elisabeth*), Raimondi (*Philip*), Valentini Terrani (*Eboli*), Nucci (*Rodrigo*), Ghiaurov (*Grand Inquisitor*), Storojev (*Monk*), Murray (*Thibault*), Auger (*Heavenly Voice*).
La Scala Ch and Orch/Abbado
Deutsche Grammophon 415 316-2 (4 CDs) R 1985

Five-act version of 1886, in Italian
Domingo (*C*), Caballé (*El*), Raimondi (*P*), Verrett (*Eb*), Milnes (*R*), Foiani (*GI*), Estes (*M*), Wallis (*T*), Del Campo (*V*).
Ambrosian Opera Ch, Royal Opera House Orch/Giulini
EMI CDS 7 47701 8 (3 CDs), EX290712-3 (3 LPs), EX290712-4 (3 cassettes)
R 1971

Five-act version of 1886, in Italian
Bergonzi (*C*), Tebaldi (*El*), Ghiaurov (*P*), Bumbry (*Eb*), Fischer-Dieskau (*R*), Talvela (*GI*), Franc (*M*), J. Sinclair (*T*), Carlyle (*V*).
Royal Opera House Ch and Orch/Solti
Decca 421 114-2 (3 CDs) R 1966

Four-act version of 1883, in Italian
Carreras (*C*), Freni (*El*), Ghiaurov (*P*), Baltsa (*Eb*), Cappuccilli (*R*), Raimondi (*GI*), van Dam (*M*), Gruberova (*T*), Hendricks (*V*).
Deutsche Oper Ch, BPO/Karajan
EMI CMS 7 69304 2 (3 CDs), EX769304-1 (3 LPs), EX769304-4 (3 cassettes)
R 1979

Four-act version of 1883, in Italian
Corelli (*C*), Janowitz (*El*), Ghiaurov (*P*), Verrett (*Eb*), Wächter (*R*), Talvela (*GI*), Franc (*M*), Gruberova (*T*), Blegen (*V*).
Vienna State Opera Ch, VPO/Stein
Rodolphe RPC 32653.55 (3 CDs) R 1970

Claudio Abbado is no stranger to the terse four-act version of *Don Carlos* — a 1968 La Scala performance may be tracked down on a Melodram import (MEL 37038) — but more recently he has preferred to present as complete a text as possible. By 1977 he had welded at least two of the crucial scenes which never reached the Paris première into the 1886 edition; a pity, then, that they are included only among the afterthoughts in the most comprehensive of the five readily available recordings. For in the case of Raimondi's older, wiser Philip, the lament for the dead Posa — the theme Verdi modified as the Requiem's Lacrimosa — is the necessary climax to a very human characterisation and one of the three cornerstones in an uneven set. The others are a Philip-Posa confrontation which grasps the political nettle, Abbado urging his La Scala players to go even further than the involved, if not always ideally steady, Leo Nucci in passionately breaking down royal reserve, and an Act Four monologue where Raimondi finds much more inwardness than in his performance for Giulini nearly fifteen years earlier (the final

The 'auto-da-fé', Metropolitan Opera, 1983, with Mirella Freni (Elisabeth), Louis Quilico (Rodrigo), Nicolai Ghiaurov (Philip), Jerome Hines (Grand Inquisitor) and Plácido Domingo (Don Carlos); 1978 producer, John Dexter, set designer, David Reppa, costume designer, Ray Diffen (photo: Winnie Klotz)

outburst, given more backbone by the French text, is magisterially moving the second time around).

Abbado also has his basses in the right roles: Ghiaurov, with his blacker, more inflexible delivery, works best as Grand Inquisitor to Raimondi's Philip, although he plays a less conscientious King on three of the other recordings. On the Karajan set, in fact, the roles are reversed — the only weakness in casting otherwise from strength. Karajan dispenses with Fontainebleau but